CROCHET AT PLAY

30 fun hats, scarves, clothes and toys for kids to enjoy

KAT GOLDIN

Kyle Books

To my four loves. You inspire me every day.

First published in Great Britain in 2013 by
Kyle Books
an imprint of Kyle Cathie Limited
67–69 Whitfield Street
London W1T 4HF
general.enquiries@kylebooks.com
www.kylebooks.com

ISBN: 978 0 85783 165 1

A CIP catalogue record for this title is available from the British Library

Kat Goldin is hereby identified as the author of this work in accordance with Section 77 of the Copyright, Designs and Patents Act 1988

Text © Kat Goldin 2013
Photographs © Kat Goldin 2013
Design © Kyle Books 2013
Illustrations © Sarah Leuzzi 2013
Technical illustrations © Kuo Kang Chen 2013

Editor: Vicky Orchard
Design: Louise Leffler
Photography: Kat Goldin
Styling: Nadine Tubbs
Technical editor: Joanne Scrace
Production: Lisa Pinell

Colour reproduction by ALTA London
Printed and bound in China by Toppan Leefung Printing Ltd.

CONTENTS

INTRODUCTION

If you were to take the contents of this book and boil them down to distil the essence of the design, you would find that the chief ingredient of every item in the book is 'fun'. From the big picture of each chapter to the finer details of the wool, stitch and construction choices, I have always tried to keep the fun-factor at the forefront of my mind:

◉ fun to make
◉ fun to wear
◉ fun to see

Making for children is one of the best excuses I know to bring a touch of whimsy and magic to designs. Small touches, like ears sewn onto the hood of a jacket, make a normal garment come alive as a thing of play.

Although I had been taught to crochet as a child, it was the birth of my son in 2007 that re-ignited my desire to pick up a hook. Every family member and friend received ill-fitting hats and scarves. As my skills grew, I struggled to find things I actually wanted to crochet. Searching for hours through books and on Ravelry, it was rare to discover patterns that were modern, gender neutral and wearable. So, I took up knitting.

And I knitted – scarves and hats and blankets and jumpers. And the more I knitted, the more I missed the portability and flexibility of crochet. Knitting needles are easily whipped out of complicated cardigans by toddlers. Stitches are missed when one's attention is diverted elsewhere. Over time, I was called back to the hook. This time, instead of looking for patterns, I decided to make my own. Influenced by knitwear design, the vibrant handmade movement and my own three small children, I have always sought to take a fresh look at crochet and its possibilities.

The patterns collected in this book are organised into four chapters:
Heads and Shoulders, for hats, scarves and capes
Fingers, Knees and Toes, for gloves, slippers and the like
Whole Self, for when you need something to put your 'whole self' in (or at least the top half)
The Play Room, a collection of designs to liven up any space for children.

Most patterns in this book are sized up to age six, with a few just for the bigger kids and a few just for babies. From small, quick, last-minute gifts to bigger projects, this book has something for all of the small people in your life.

Happy crocheting (and most importantly, have fun!).

Kat
www.slugsontherefrigerator.com

GETTING STARTED

YARNS

When buying yarn, my advice is to buy the best you can afford. Children's items are small and require relatively little in the way of yarn, so it is a good excuse for paying a bit more for wool that will stand the test of time (and hand-me-downs) and will be enjoyable to wear and work with.

Walking into your local yarn or craft store, it is easy to be overwhelmed by the array of colours, fibres and weights of wool available. I have tried to choose yarns that not only look good, but also are relatively kid-proof, with a lot of washable choices and suggested alternatives.

Acrylic

There is no doubt that acrylic is the cheapest available. Inexpensive and often very soft, acrylic has become a go-to fibre for children's wear. However, acrylic yarns often don't wear well, and they can result in pilled and misshapen garments.

Wool

Scratchy wool jumpers from your grandma are a thing of the past (hopefully!) Wool yarns, especially merino wool, can be gorgeous and soft and light. There are many machine washable wool yarns on the market. Look for 'superwash' on the label, particularly if you are making something as a gift. It means your lovingly handmade present is more likely to be worn. Superwash merino is one of my favourite fibres to work with.

Other Fibres

From cotton to bamboo to alpaca to milk fibres, there are an astounding number of yarns available. Cotton and bamboo yarns are excellent choices for children. They are usually machine washable and are great for layering. Other fibres each have their own properties. If you have questions about how a yarn will behave, ask a member of staff at your local store for advice.

Substituting Yarn

In each pattern throughout the book, I have suggested a yarn that works well for the pattern in terms of weight, drape and washability. I have also given a few suggestions to help you find some other alternatives. In each pattern I have also included the amount of yarn required, the yarn's properties and the weight. To ensure you are successful in substituting yarn, choose something similar.

HOOKS

Crochet hooks can be made from an endless variety of materials – wood, acrylic, aluminium, steel, to name a few. Personally, I prefer the glide and feel of aluminium crochet hooks, as they are both affordable and work with most wools. However, it may take some time to figure out which kind you prefer, so try a few and see.

Crochet hooks are sized in relation to their diameter. A larger crochet hook will take more yarn into the stitch. Most of the time larger hooks are used with heavier yarn and smaller hooks with finer weights.

OTHER SUPPLIES

Tapestry/Yarn Needles

These have large eyes and are blunt.

Stitch Markers

Use the types that have a split ring or are open, as you will need to move them with each round. I often use just a scrap of yarn or a safety pin as a stitch marker, rather than buying anything special.

Sewing Needle

Used particularly for sewing on buttons. These are thinner and sharper than yarn needles. If you don't have co-ordinating thread for buttons, split your yarn lengthwise to thread through your sewing needle to sew on buttons.

Scissors

Sharp embroidery scissors are particularly useful for crochet, allowing you to make precision cuts without a lot of bulk getting in the way.

Buttons

Possibly my favourite part of making a garment is choosing the buttons. Remember that buttons can be choking hazards, so ensure they are sewn on very tightly and are checked regularly.

SIZING

All the finished garments in this book have detailed measurements. Each measurement has a guide for the age range the item will fit. Please remember that these are only guides, and that children come in all sorts of sizes. Use the actual measurements of the recipient to decide which 'age' to make. The major measurements, such as chest and length, are given at the beginning of each pattern.
- Head Circumference: Measure around head, just above their ears.
- Chest: Measure around the child's trunk, under their armpits.
- Sleeve Length: Measure from their shoulder to their wrist.
- Length: Measure from the back of their neck to their waist.
- Waist: Measure around their natural waist.
- Hand Length: Measure from their wrist to middle finger.
- Hand Width: Measure across the palm of the hand, just under their fingers.

- Foot Length: Measure from their toe to heel.
- Foot Width: Measure across the ball of their foot.

The finished chest measurement of a garment, such as a cardigan or jacket, should be 5–10cm larger than the child's actual chest measurements. Hats should be slightly smaller than their head circumference and tend to fit a large range of head sizes.

If you are making for a baby that hasn't been born yet, think about when the baby is due to arrive and how old they might be when they need the item you are making. If in doubt, size up.

Items in this book are generally sized large to make sure that there is plenty of room to grow.

TENSION

Everyone crochets slightly differently. Some people work very loosely, some more tightly. For items such as scarves and home accessories, tension isn't that critical, as you will just end up with a slightly bigger (or smaller) blanket. However, to ensure that your garments fit, you need to ensure you are working to the specified tension.

At the most basic level, tension is the number of stitches and rows in a 10cm square. Each pattern in this book will give you the information as to how many stitches and how many rows (or rounds) it will take to make a 10cm square with your selected yarn and suggested hook.

To see how your tension matches with the suggested one, make at least a 10cm square with the suggested hook in the indicated stitch pattern. Then, if you plan to wash your finished item (which will be in most cases), wash and block (see page 14) your swatch as you intend to wash your finished object. Let it dry completely and then measure your stitches and rows.

If you measure more stitches and rows in the swatch than the suggested tension, switch to a larger hook. If you measure fewer stitches and rows in the swatch than the suggested tension, switch to a smaller hook. Then, make another swatch and wash it, as you did the first to double-check your tension.

TECHNIQUES AND BASIC STITCHES

HOLDING YOUR HOOK AND YARN

Crochet hooks are sometimes held like a pencil, with your forefinger and thumb placed over the flattened portion of the hook, and with the end of the hook coming out over your thumb. Hooks can also be held like a knife, with the end of the hook under your hand.

The yarn should be held in the opposite hand to the hook. It helps to thread the wool through your fingers to create a bit of tension and give you better control of your work.

It will take some time to find what is most comfortable for you. If you are just starting out, choose a project that uses a heavier weight yarn and larger hook to make it easier to get to grips with the basic techniques.

Hook held like a pencil

Hook held like a knife

SLIP KNOT

Leaving a 15cm tail, take the yarn and make a loop, crossing the cut end of the wool under the ball end of the wool. Reach through the loop with your hook and catch the ball end of the wool with your hook. Pull through the original loop. Pull both ends of the yarn to tighten.

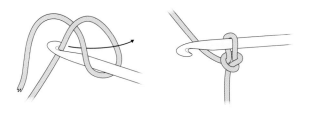

CHAIN STITCH (CH)

Begin with a slip knot on your hook and place your yarn over the hook. Twisting your hook slightly, draw your yarn through the loop on your hook. Repeat as many times as required.

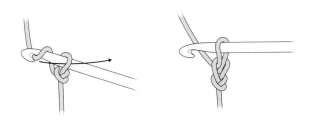

COUNTING CHAIN STITCHES

When counting how many stitches you have made, do not count the knot or the loop on your hook.

TURNING CHAINS

In order to get your new row or round up to the correct height, you will often be called to make a turning chain. These are chain stitches at the beginning of each row or round. Usually, you count the turning chain as a stitch, except in the case of double crochet. However, each pattern will tell you whether the turning chains are counted or not.

Crochet stitches are different heights. Each stitch has a corresponding number of turning chains made at the beginning of the round/row:

1ch = Double crochet
2ch = Half treble crochet
3ch = Treble crochet
4ch = Triple treble crochet

Sometimes you will be called on to chain more than the number required for the stitch, in which case that will count as a stitch plus a number of chains.

ANATOMY OF A CROCHET STITCH

Loops

At the top of the crochet stitch, you will see two loops, or a 'V' that is left after you have made the stitch. Unless otherwise stated, always work into both loops.

Post

The 'body' of the stitch. This is the portion of the stitch that is made of yarn overs. The more yarn overs in a stitch means a taller post.

Fork

This is the bottom portion of the stitch that connects it to the previous round or row.

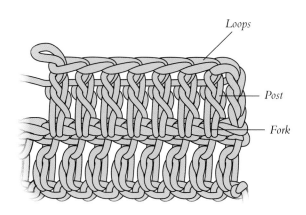

SLIP STITCH (slst)

Slip stitches are most often used for joining rounds or for moving the working yarn to a new point on the garment without having to add bulky stitches or break the yarn.

1. Insert the hook into the stitch.
2. Place the yarn over the hook.
3. Pull through both the stitch and the loop on the hook.

DOUBLE CROCHET (dc)

1. Insert the hook into the stitch.
2. Place the yarn over the hook.
3. Pull through the stitch.
4. Yarn over the hook again.
5. Pull through the two loops on the hook.

HALF TREBLE CROCHET (htr)

1. Place the yarn over the hook.
2. Insert the hook into the stitch.
3. Place the yarn over the hook.
4. Pull through the stitch (three loops on hook).
5. Yarn over the hook again.
6. Pull through all three loops on your hook.

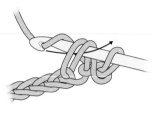

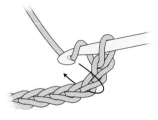

Moving yarn

Joining in the round

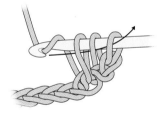

TREBLE CROCHET (tr)

1. Place the yarn over the hook.
2. Insert the hook into the stitch.
3. Place the yarn over the hook.
4. Pull through the stitch (three loops on hook).
5. Yarn over the hook again.
6. Pull through two loops on your hook (two loops on hook).
7. Yarn over again.
8. Pull through the last two loops on the hook.

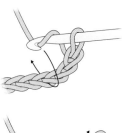

DOUBLE TREBLE CROCHET (dtr)

1. Place the yarn over the hook twice.
2. Insert the hook into the stitch.
3. Place the yarn over the hook.
4. Pull through the stitch (four loops on hook).
5. Yarn over the hook again.
6. Pull through two loops on the hook (three loops on hook).
7. Yarn over the hook again.
8. Pull through two loops on the hook (two loops on hook).
9. Yarn over again.
10. Pull through the last two loops on the hook.

RAISED STITCHES

Raised stitches are used in cable crochet and for making ribbing. They are made by working around the post/body of the stitch, instead of the top of the stitch. Raised stitches can be made with any of the basic stitches, but are most often used with treble crochet.

RAISED TREBLE FRONT (RtrF)

1. Place the yarn over the hook.
2. Insert the hook into the space between the stitch you are raising and the previous stitch, from the front of your work.
3. Bring the hook around the back of the stitch and through to the front of your work in between the stitch and the next stitch.
4. Yarn over hook.
5. Pull the loop back through the spaces between the stitches.
6. Yarn over and pull through two loops twice, as you would a normal treble crochet.

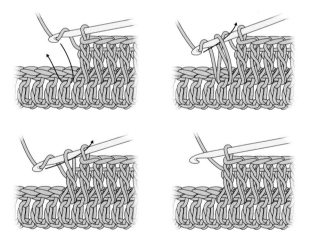

RAISED TREBLE BACK (RtrB)

1. Place the yarn over the hook.
2. Bring the hook to the back of your work and insert the hook into the space between the stitch you are raising and the previous stitch, from the back of your work.
3. Bring the hook around the front of the stitch and through to the back of your work in between the stitch and the next stitch.
4. Yarn over hook.
5. Pull the loop back through the spaces between the stitches.
6. Yarn over and pull through two loops twice, as you would a normal treble crochet.

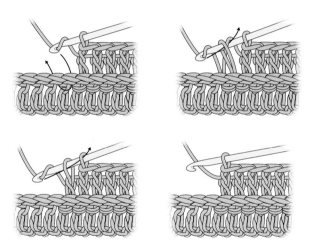

CABLED CROCHET

Cables are achieved in crochet by crossing groups of raised stitches. It can be tricky to understand at first. In all of the cables worked in this book, you will miss a specified number of stitches, work a group of raised stitches, then go back and work the missed stitches so they cross over the front of the cable. You then continue working as normal in the pattern.

FOUNDATION DOUBLE CROCHET (fdc)

Foundation crochet or chainless crochet is a way of working a starting row without having to work a chain. This is used in places where you need more stretch than a chain stitch can provide.

1. Starting with a slip knot, chain two.
2. Insert the hook back into the first chain.
3. Yarn over and pull through (two loops on hook).
4. Yarn over and pull through one loop on your hook (two loops on hook). This counts as your chain stitch.
5. Yarn over again and pull through the remaining two loops on the hook.

To continue:

1. Insert the hook into the chain stitch of the previous fdc.
2. Yarn over and pull through (two loops on hook). This counts as your joining stitch.
3. Yarn over and pull through one loop on your hook (two loops on hook). This counts as your chain stitch.
4. Yarn over again and pull through the remaining two loops on the hook.

DECREASES

Decreases are made by working the specified stitch up to the last yarn over, then inserting the hook into the next stitch, working it up to the last yarn over. Then yarn over and pull through all the loops on the hook.

WORKING IN THE ROUND

Of all the patterns in this book, most call for starting working in the round with a magic loop (also called adjustable loop). This is my preferred way of starting, as it enables you to get a very tight, closed first round.

1. Make a loop with the yarn, placing the cut end behind the ball end of the wool.
2. Reach through the loop with your hook, catch the ball end of the yarn with your hook and pull through the original loop. Do not pull tight.
3. Chain the specified number of stitches. This will help secure the loop.
4. Make the specified stitches, working into the large loop at the bottom of your work.
5. Pull the tail end tightly to bring the bottom of the stitches into a circle.
6. After you have worked a few rounds of the pattern, tie off the tail end to prevent the magic loop from opening back up.

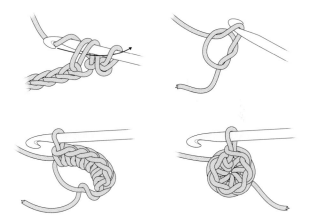

Alternatively, if you find the magic loop difficult, you can begin working in the round with four chains. Join with a slip stitch in the round and work your pattern into the loop created by the ring of chain stitched (not working into the individual chains, as you would when working flat).

JOINING YARNS

To join a new colour or ball of wool seamlessly to your work, switch your yarn at the last yarn over of the stitch. For example, if I were switching when using double crochet, I would:

1. Insert the hook into the stitch.
2. Place the yarn over the hook.
3. Pull through the stitch.
4. Yarn over the hook again with the new colour/yarn.
5. Pull through the two loops on the hook.

You can easily work in any ends of yarn by working around them as you continue down the round/row. Simply lay them across the top of the row you are working on and continue crocheting into the stitches as normal.

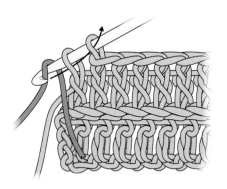

FINISHING

Once you reach the end of your work, cut the yarn, leaving at least a 15cm tail for weaving in. Pull the cut end through the last loop that remained on your hook to stop your stitches from unravelling. If there are yarn ends that you have not been able to work in as described above, use a tapestry needle to weave the remaining ends securely into the back of your work. Weaving them into 3–4 stitches in 3–4 different directions will ensure they do not pop out later.

WASHING AND BLOCKING

Always use the ball band for your yarn as a guide to how to care for your final garment. Many will say 'Hand Wash Only'. However, if your machine has it, it is often OK to use a wool cycle on most handmade items. Test your swatch first!

When working with wools that have a high natural fibre content, you are able to block your project, which will help the yarn relax into the shape you have made. There are many different blocking techniques. Steam blocking uses an iron with a high steam setting. Gently press your work (not too hard or you will flatten the stitches).

I normally use wet blocking. This can take longer to dry, but does tend to give the most consistent results.

1. Wet your work in lukewarm water with a bit of wool wash in it.
2. Gently agitate your work (not too hard - you don't want it to felt!)

3. Rinse in cool water and gently press the water out.
4. Lay your work flat on a towel and roll up to get more water out.
5. Lay the item out on a flat surface. It may help to pin the edges down to help it stay in shape.
6. Leave to fully dry.

SEWING UP
Slip Stitch Seams

Using a slip stitch to join different parts of an object creates a very strong seam. Line up the stitches of the two pieces you are joining and insert the hook through all four loops of the stitches, yarn over hook, and pull through the two pieces you are joining and the loop on the hook. Repeat to the end of the seam.

EMBROIDERY

A few of the patterns in the book call for a small amount of embroidery and hand sewing.

Slip Stitch Embroidery (Surface Crochet)

Working on the outside of your work, insert the hook into the space between the crochet stitch you wish to work from. Bring the hook out into an adjacent space, in the direction you wish to work in. Yarn over and pull through. Insert the hook into the next space between the crochet stitch you wish to work from. Bring the hook out through an adjacent space, in the direction you wish to work in. Yarn over and pull through the stitch and the loop on the hook. Repeat as required.

Running Stitch

Thread a needle with yarn and work up and down through the crochet fabric with even spaces between the stitches.

Backstitch

Backstitch is similar to running stitch, except you will work a portion of the stitches back on themselves. Pull the stitch through the crochet fabric and then back into the underside behind where the thread came out. The needle is carried under the fabric to the point of the new stitch, where it is brought up again and back to where the thread was brought up on the last stitch.

READING A PATTERN

I like to think of patterns as reading a code. It can be tricky at first, but patterns are written using standard abbreviations for stitches and what to do. Know the code and you've got it!

Stitch or instruction	Abbreviation
Back Loop Only	BLO
Chain	ch
Chain Space	chsp
Decreasing	dec
Double Crochet	dc
Double Treble	dtr
Front Loop Only	FLO
Foundation Crochet	fwxx
Half Treble	htr
Increasing	inc
Raised Back	RxxB
Raised Front	RxxF
Rounds	rnd
Rows	row
Slipstitch	slst
Starting Chain	stch
Stitches	sts
Treble	tr
Treble/Triple Treble	ttr
Turning Chain	tch
Work 2 x Together	x2tog
Yarn Over	YO

Pattern Basics

Example: Rows 2 (4, 6) – 7 (9, 11, -): 1ch, [2dc in dc, 2dc] three times, 2 (3, 4, -) dc, ★2dc in dc; repeat from ★ to end. Join. Turn. 20 (21, 22, -)dc.

• Numbers in brackets relate to the instructions for the various sizes from smallest to largest, working left to right. Can be row or round numbers, stitch counts or repeats.

• The symbol '-' in place of any instruction for a particular size means that size isn't worked in that portion of the instructions.

• The instruction '2dc in dc, 2dc' means make two double crochet in the next double crochet stitch, then double crochet in the next two stitches.

• Instructions in square brackets are to be repeated a set number of times, as directed immediately following the second bracket. There may be variations relating to the size, in which case follow the appropriate number in normal brackets.

• When instructions are proceeded by a ★, this means to repeat that sequence of stitches as many times as indicated, usually to the end of the round or row.

• 'Join' means to join the round, unless otherwise instructed, by working a slip stitch into the first stitch of the round.

• 'Turn' means to turn your work.

• The stitch counts at the end of the row tell you how many stitches you should have worked in that row or round.

HEAD AND SHOULDERS

ACORN

Inspired by my own childhood collecting baskets of acorns from our oak trees. This deeply textured hat looks complicated, but a few basic stitches combined with a zigzag pattern make it an interesting, but simple make.

skill level: intermediate

Size	Baby	Toddler	4+ years
Finished circumference	31cm	38cm	46cm
Finished height	14cm	17cm	19cm
Yarn amounts	60m	90m	120m

MATERIALS:
- 1 x 100g hank of Cascade 220 (100 per cent wool), 201m, Vandyke Brown (7822)
- 5mm/H8 hook
- Tapestry needle

YARN REVIEW:
You would be hard-pressed to find a range of yarns with the colour options that are available with Cascade 220. This worsted-weight yarn's good stitch definition and wearability make it an excellent option for outerwear.

YARN ALTERNATIVES:
Malabrigo Worsted
Quince and Co. Lark

TENSION:
Work 15sts and eight rows in treble crochet to measure 10cm square using 5mm hook, or size required to obtain tension.

SPECIAL STITCH PATTERNS:
Puff Stitch (PS)
[YO, insert the hook into the stitch and draw up a loop] twice (five loops on hook). YO and pull through four loops on hook. YO and pull through last two loops on hook.

Pattern notes: This is a very stretchy pattern where each size will fit a range of head sizes. Do not turn your work at the end of each round.

INSTRUCTIONS:

Make 4ch. Join in the round.

Round 1: 4ch (counts as 1tr and 1ch), 2tr, [1tr, ch, 2tr] four times. Join into 3rd ch of stch. (15) sts.

Round 2: (from Round 3 on, the 2ch at the beginning of the rounds do not count as a st) 2ch, ★(PS, 1ch, PS) into chsp, miss 1tr, 3tr into tr, miss 1tr; repeat from ★ to end. Join into the 1st chsp. (25) sts.

Round 3: 2ch, ★(PS, 1ch, PS) into chsp, 1RtrF into tr, 3tr into next tr, 1RtrF into next tr; repeat from ★ to end. Join into the 1st chsp. (35) sts.

For sizes Toddler and 4+ years ONLY

Round 4: 2ch, ★(PS, 1ch, PS) into chsp, 1RtrF into next 2 sts, 3tr into next tr, 1RtrF into next 2 sts; repeat from ★ to end. Join into the 1st chsp. - (45, 45) sts.

For size 4+ years ONLY

Round 5: 2ch, ★(PS, 1ch, PS) into chsp, 1RtrF into next 3 sts, 3tr into the next tr, 1RtrF into the next 3 sts; repeat from ★ to end. Join into the 1st chsp. - (-, 55) sts.

For ALL sizes

Round 4 (5, 6) – 9 (12, 15): 2ch, ★(PS, 1ch, PS) into chsp; miss 1 RtrF, 1RtrF into the next 1 (2, 3) sts, 3tr into the next tr, 1RtrF into the next 1 (2, 3) sts, miss one RtrF; repeat from ★ to end. Join into the 1st chsp. 35 (45, 55) sts.

For size Baby ONLY

Round 10: ★(PS, 1ch, PS) into chsp, 1RtrF, 3RhtrF, 1RtrF; repeat from ★ to end. Join. Break yarn and weave in ends. (35) sts.

For size Toddler ONLY

Round 13: ★(PS, 1ch, PS) into chsp, 1RttrF, 1RtrF, 3RhtrF, 1RtrF, 1RttrF; repeat from ★ to end. Join. Break yarn and weave in ends. (45) sts.

For size 4+ years ONLY

Round 16: ★(PS, 1ch, PS) into chsp. 2RttrF, 1RtrF, 3RhtrF, 1RtrF, 2RttrF★ repeat from ★ to end. Join. Break yarn and weave in ends. (55) sts.

Stem (All sizes)

Make 2ch, 3dc into a magic loop. (4)

Round 1–4: (you will work in a spiral) 4dc. (4)

Fasten off, leaving a 30cm tail. Using the tail, sew onto the top of the hat.

CROWN

A quick and easy make for your little royalty.

Size	Newborn	Baby	Toddler	4+ years
Circumference	30.5cm	35.5cm	43cm	48cm
Yarn amounts	19m	26m	36.5m	45.5m

MATERIALS:
- 1 x 25g ball of Sublime Lustrous Extra Fine Merino (67 per cent extra fine merino, 33 per cent nylon), 95m Flinty (259)
- Also pictured 1 x ball of Sublime Lustrous Extra Fine Merino (67 per cent extra fine merino, 33 per cent nylon), 95m Truffle (289)
- 3.75mm/F5 hook
- Tapestry needle

YARN REVIEW:
Soft and luxurious, this DK wool not only looks lovely, but also will make your little one feel like royalty.

YARN ALTERNATIVES:
James C Brett Twinkle DK

TENSION:
Work 21 sts and 12 rows to measure 10cm square using 3.75mm hook, or size required to obtain tension.

PATTERN NOTES:
- This pattern can easily be sized up or down by altering the number of chain stitches in multiples of eight.
- Do not count the 1ch at the beginning of the round as a stitch.
- Do not turn your work at the end of each round.

INSTRUCTIONS:

Make 64 (72, 88, 96) chain. Join in the round.

Rounds 1–4 (5, 6, 7): 1ch, 64 (72, 88, 96) dc. Join. 64 (72, 88, 96)dc.

Round 5 (6, 7, 8): (3ch (counts as 1tr), 3tr, 2ch, 4tr) into dc, miss 3, 1dc, miss 3 ★(4tr, 2ch, 4tr) into dc, miss 3, 1dc, miss 3; repeat from ★ to end. Join. 8 (9, 11, 12) treble stitch clusters.

Break yarn and weave in ends.

FLAT CAP

Perfect for walking out on the moors or toddling out at the park.

skill level: beginner

Size	Newborn	Baby	Toddler	4+ years
Circumference	35cm	39cm	42cm	47cm
Length	18cm	19cm	20cm	22.5cm
Yarn amounts	47m	54m	70.5m	81.5m

MATERIALS:
- 1 x 50g ball of Debbie Bliss Donegal Luxury Tweed Aran (90 per cent wool, 10 per cent Angora), 88m Chocolate (360014)
- 5mm/H8 hook
- 4mm/G6 hook
- Tapestry needle
- 32 (36, 39, 44)cm of fine elastic cord, tied or sewn into a loop

YARN REVIEW:
The touch of Angora in this tweed makes it a very soft and wearable yarn.

YARN ALTERNATIVES:
Rowan Felted Tweed Aran
Patons Soft Tweed Aran

TENSION:
Work 14 sts and ten rows in pattern to measure 10cm square using 5mm hook, or size needed to obtain tension.

PATTERN:
Row 1: 1ch (does not count as a stitch), dc across.
Row 2: 3ch (counts as 1tr), tr across. Line up working edge of the brim with the stitches not worked at the front flap of the hat, upside down, RS facing. Place your elastic loop on top of your work and work around it as you slst brim to the underside of the hat. This will help the hat stay on.

PATTERN NOTES:
• This hat has a slightly unusual construction. You will start at the front flap, working in rounds, then only work with half of the stitches in rows to the back of the head. You will join the brim on after the rest of the hat is complete.

- Count the 3ch at the beginning of tr rounds/rows as a stitch.
- Do NOT count the 1ch at the beginning of dc rounds/rows as a stitch.

Front Flap

With larger hook, make 11 (11, 13, 15)ch.

Round 1: Starting in the 2nd chain from hook, 2dc into the same ch, 8 (8, 10, 12)dc, 4dc into the last stitch, turning as you go to work into the other side of the chain, 8 (8, 10, 12)dc, 2dc into the first stitch (this stitch already has 2dc in it). Join into the 1st dc. 24 (24, 28, 32)dc.

Round 2: 3ch, 2tr in the next stitch, 8 (8, 10, 12)tr, 2tr in the next stitch, 2tr, 2tr in the next stitch, 8 (8, 10, 12)tr, 2tr in the next stitch, 1tr. Join. 28 (28, 32, 36)dc.

Round 3: 1ch, 2dc into the tch of the previous round, 2dc in the next stitch, 8 (8, 10, 12)dc, 2dc in the next stitch, 4dc, 2dc in the next stitch, 8 (8, 10, 12)dc, 2dc in the next stitch, 2dc. Join. 32 (32, 36, 40)dc.

For Newborn and Baby sizes, go to 'Top' Section.

For sizes Toddler and 4+ years ONLY

Round 4: 3ch, 2tr, 2tr in the next stitch, - (-, 10, 12)tr, 2tr in the next stitch, 6tr, 2tr in the next stitch, - (-, 10, 12)tr, 2tr in the next stitch, 3tr. Join. - (-, 40, 44)dc.

Round 5: 1ch, 4dc, 2dc in the next stitch, - (-, 10, 12)dc, 2dc in the next stitch, 8dc, 2dc in the next stitch, - (-, 10, 12)dc, 2dc in the next stitch, 4dc. Join. -, (-, 44, 48)dc.

Top
For ALL sizes

This section extends half of the front flap stitches in rows to the back of the hat.

Row 1(RS): 3ch, 15 (15, 21, 23)tr. Turn. 16 (16, 22, 24)tr.

Row 2: 1ch, 1dc, 2dc in the next stitch, dc to 2 stitches from end, 2dc in next stitch, 1dc. Turn. 18 (18, 24, 26)dc.

Row 3: 3ch, 2tr into the next stitch, tr to 2 stitches from end, 2tr in next stitch, 1tr. Turn. 20 (20, 26, 28)tr.

Rows 4–9 (11, 11, 13): Repeat rows 2–3. Turn. 32 (38, 42, 48)tr.

Row 10 (12, 12, 14): 1ch, dc2tog across. Turn. 16 (19, 21, 24)dc.

Row 11 (13, 13, 15): 3ch, 15 (18, 20, 23)tr. Turn. 16 (19, 21, 24)tr.

Row 12 (14, 14, 16): 1ch, 0 (1, 1, 0)dc, dc2tog across. Turn. 8 (10, 11, 12)dc.

Row 13 (15, 15, 17): 3ch, 7 (9, 10, 11)tr. Turn. 8 (10, 11, 12)tr.

Fold the last row in half, right sides together, lining up the stitches. Slst through all four loops along. Break yarn and weave in ends.

Brim

With smaller hook, make 11 (11, 13, 15)ch.

Row 1: Starting in the 2nd chain from the hook, 10 (10, 12, 14)dc. Turn. 10 (10, 12, 14)dc.

Rows 2–4 (4, 6, 6): 1ch, 1dc, 2dc in the next stitch, dc to 2 stitches from end, 2dc in next stitch, 1dc. Turn.

Row 5 (5, 7, 7) – 6 (6, 8, 8): 1ch, 16 (16, 22, 24)dc. Turn. 16 (16, 22, 24)dc. Line up working edge of brim with the

stitches not worked at the front flap of the hat, upside down, RS facing. Slst brim to the underside of the hat.

Edging

Round 1: Continuing with the smaller hook and working around the elastic as you go, 26 (30, 30, 34)htr around the underside edge of the hat back around to the brim, 1dc into every other row down the side of the brim, 10 (10, 12, 14)dc across the front of the brim, 1dc into every other row down the other side of the brim. Do not turn, do not join. 26 (30, 30, 34)htr and 16 (16, 20, 22)dc.

Round 2: 6 (7, 7, 8)htr, htr2tog, 3 (4, 4, 5)htr, htr3tog, 3 (4, 4, 5)htr, htr2tog, 6 (7, 7, 8)htr. Do not work into the brim. Break yarn and weave in ends. 22 (26, 26, 30)htr.

FLOWER AND BUD HAT

Little clusters of puff stitches have always been my favourite crochet stitch. They remind me of springtime buds, just waiting to pop open.

skill level: beginner

Size	Newborn	Baby	Toddler	4+ years
Circumference	30.5cm	35.5cm	43cm	48cm
Height	11.5cm	13cm	16cm	19cm
Yarn amounts	45m	59m	87m	115m

MATERIALS:

- Main Colour (MC): 1 x 50g ball of Sirdar Simply Recycled DK (51 per cent recycled cotton, 49 per cent acrylic), 130m Grey (0018)
- Contrast Colour (CC): 1 x 50g ball of Sirdar Simply Recycled DK (51 per cent recycled cotton, 49 per cent acrylic), 130m Mustard (0019)
- 3.75mm/F5 hook
- Tapestry needle

YARN REVIEW:

The recycled cotton in this DK-weight yarn is lovely and soft, making a perfect springtime hat.

YARN ALTERNATIVES:

Rowan Hand Knit DK Cotton
Wendy Supreme DK Cotton

TENSION:

Work five pattern repeats and seven rows in pattern to measure 10cm square using 3.75mm hook, or size required to obtain tension.

SPECIAL STITCHES:

Puff Stitch (PS)

[YO, insert the hook into the stitch and draw up a loop] three times (seven loops on hook). YO and pull through six loops on hook. YO and pull through last two loops on hook.

Pattern notes: Do not count the 2ch at the beginning of the round as a stitch. Do not turn your work at the end of the rounds.

PATTERN:
[PS, 2ch, PS] into the 2chsp between the PS cluster of the previous round.

INSTRUCTIONS:
Using MC, 2ch, [PS, 2ch] six times into a magic loop. Join. (6).
Round 1: 2ch, [(PS, 2ch, PS) into 2chsp, (PS, 2ch, PS, 2ch, PS) into 2chsp] three times. Join. (15)PS.
Round 2: 2ch, [(PS, 2ch, PS, 2ch, PS) into 2chsp, (PS, 2ch, PS) into 2chsp twice] three times. Join. (21)PS.
Round 3: [(PS, 2ch, PS) into 2chsp three times, (PS, 2ch, PS, 2ch, PS) into 2chsp] three times. Join. (27)PS.

For Newborn size, go to Row 7.

For sizes Baby, Toddler and 4+ years ONLY
Round 4: 2ch, [(PS, 2ch, PS, 2ch, PS) into the next 2chsp, (PS, 2ch, PS) into 2chsp four times] three times. - (33, 33, 33)PS.

For Baby size, go to Row 7.

For sizes Toddler and 4+ years ONLY
Round 5: [(PS, 2ch, PS) into 2chsp five times, (PS, 2ch, PS, 2ch, PS) into 2chsp] three times. Join. - (-, 39, 39) PS.
For Toddler size, go to Row 7.

For size 4+ years ONLY
Round 6: 2ch, [(PS, 2ch, PS, 2ch, PS) into 2chsp, (PS, 2ch, PS) into 2chsp six times] three times. - (-, -, 45)PS.

For ALL sizes
Round 7: (For Newborn and Baby, work this round in CC, for Toddler and 4+ work in MC) 2ch, (PS, 2ch, PS) in each 2chsp around. 30 (36, 42, 48)PS.
Round 8: (For Newborn and Baby, work this round in MC, for Toddler and 4+ work in CC) 2ch, (PS, 2ch, PS) in each 2chsp around. 30 (36, 42, 48)PS.
Round 9: Repeat round 7.
Round 10: Repeat round 8.

For Newborn and Baby sizes, go to Edging.

For sizes Toddler and 4+ years ONLY
Round 11: Repeat round 7.
For Toddler size, go to Edging.

For size 4+ years ONLY
Round 12: Repeat round 7.

Edging
For ALL sizes
Round 1: Using MC, 1ch, ★1dc, 1ch, 1dc into the 2ch space, miss 1; repeat from ★ around. (Do not join. You will work in a spiral. Use a stitch marker to mark the beginning of the round.) 30 (36, 42, 48).
Rounds 2–3 (3, 5, 5): ★1dc into the next chsp, 1ch; repeat from ★ around. 30 (36, 42, 48).
Break yarn and weave in ends.

Flower (Make 2)
Round 1: Using the CC, 2ch, 4dc into a magic loop. Join. (4)dc.
Round 2: [(3ch, PS, 3ch, slst) into st] five times. You will work the last petal into the same dc as the first petal. Break yarn, leaving a 20cm tail for sewing. Using photo for placement, sew onto hat. (5) petals.

FLOWER AND BUD COWL

A complementary project to the Flower and Bud Hat, this cowl is made up of a pattern of puff stitch clusters and granite stitch.

skill level: beginner

Size	Small	Medium	Large
Circumference	45.5cm	51cm	56cm
Height	12.7cm	12.7cm	16cm
Yarn amounts	52m	58m	80m

MATERIALS:
- Main Colour (MC): 1 x 50g ball of Sirdar Simply Recycled DK (51 per cent recycled cotton, 49 per cent acrylic), 130m Grey (0018)
- Contrast Colour (CC): Small amount of Sirdar Simply Recycled DK (51 per cent recycled cotton, 49 per cent acrylic), 130m Mustard (0019)
- 3.75mm/F5 hook
- Tapestry needle

YARN REVIEW:
This DK-weight yarn is light enough for cool spring and autumn days.

YARN ALTERNATIVES:
Rowan Hand Knit DK Cotton
Wendy Supreme DK Cotton

TENSION:
Work five pattern repeats and seven rows in pattern to measure 10cm square using 3.75mm hook, or size required to obtain tension.

SPECIAL STITCHES:
Puff Stitch (PS)
[YO, insert the hook into the stitch and draw up a loop] three times (seven loops on hook). YO and pull through six loops on hook. YO and pull through last two loops on hook.

PATTERN:
[PS, 2ch, PS] into the 2chsp between the PS cluster of the previous round.

Pattern notes: This is a quick little pattern that can be made to many different variations, even sized up or down by simply chaining multiples of eight and adding or subtracting pattern repeats.

Do not count the chain stitches at the beginning of the round as a stitch.

Do not turn your work at the end of each round.

INSTRUCTIONS:

Using MC, make 72 (80, 88)ch. Join to work in the round.

Round 1: 1ch, ★1dc, 1ch, miss 1ch; repeat from ★ to end. Join. 36 (40, 44)dc.

Round 2: 1ch, ★1dc into the chsp, 1ch, miss the next stitch; repeat from ★ to end. Join. 36 (40, 44)dc.

Round 3: 3ch, ★miss [1dc, 1ch, 1dc], [PS, 2ch, PS] into chsp; repeat from ★ to end. Join. 36 (40, 44)dc.

Round 4: 1ch, ★1dc, 1ch, 1dc into the 2chsp, miss 1; repeat from ★ to end. Join. 36 (40, 44)dc.

Round 5: 1ch, ★1dc into the chsp, 1ch, miss 1; repeat from ★ to end. Join. 36 (40, 44)dc.

Work rounds 2–5 four (four, five) times.

Work round 5 one final time. Break yarn and weave in ends.

FOX STOLE

It came as a huge shock to me when I first moved to the UK that foxes aren't just adorable wild creatures that live in forests, but also pests that live in cities. I don't care and love them anyway.

skill level: intermediate

Size	Small	Medium	Large
Length	97cm	103cm	111cm
Yarn amounts	163m	167.5m	173.5m

MATERIALS:
- Main Colour (MC): 2 x 50g balls of Adriafil Regina (100 per cent wool), 125m (Rust 049)
- White: 1 x 50g ball of Adriafil Regina (100 per cent wool), 125m (White 01)
- Black: 1 x 50g ball of Adriafil Regina (100 per cent wool), 125m (Black 02)
- You only need very small amounts of the white and black, so you may consider using yarn you already have in your stash.
- 5mm/H8 hook
- 2 x buttons (1cm diameter)
- Tapestry needle

YARN REVIEW:
With a wide variety of colours and at a very affordable price, this superwash DK wool is perfect for making something that is going to keep little people warm and stylish all winter.

YARN ALTERNATIVES:
King Cole Merino Blend DK

TENSION:
Make 6.5 sts and ten rows to measure 10cm square using 5mm hook, or size required to obtain tension.

SPECIAL STITCHES:
Wattle Stitch
[dc, htr, tr] in the same stitch, miss 2.

PATTERN NOTES:
This scarf is sized only by adding length to the red section of the scarf, making it easy to size up to an adult length.

INSTRUCTIONS:

Fox Face

Starting with MC, 2ch (does not count as a stitch), 8htr into a magic loop. Join. (8)htr.

Round 1: 2ch, 2htr in each stitch around. Join. (16)htr.

Round 2: 2ch, [1htr, 2htr in the next stitch] eight times. Join. (24)htr.

Round 3: 2ch, [2htr, 2htr in the next stitch] eight times. Join. (32)htr.

Round 4: 2ch, [3htr, 2htr in the next stitch] seven times, 4htr, 4fdc, 1ch, working down the other side of the fdc, 2dc into the first stitch, 3dc, 1htr into the same stitch as the last htr that was made. Join. Do not turn. (49) sts.

Round 5: 1ch, [4dc, 2dc in the next stitch] twice, 5dc, 2fdc, 2ch, working down the other side of the fdc, 2dc, 1dc into the same dc that you started the fdc from, 4dc, 2dc in the next stitch, 5dc, 2fdc, 2ch, working down the other side of the fdc, 2dc, 1dc into the same dc that you started the fdc from, [4dc, 2dc in the next stitch] twice, 7dc, 2dc in the next stitch, 3ch, 2dc in the next stitch, 5dc. Join. Do not turn. (66) sts.

Round 6: 1ch, [5dc, 2dc in the next stitch] two times, 7dc, [1dc, 3ch, 1dc] into the 2chsp, 8dc, 2dc in the next stitch, 7dc, [1dc, 3ch, 1dc] into the 2chsp, 8dc, 2dc in the next stitch, 5dc, 2dc in the next stitch, 8dc, switch to black, carrying the MC under the back as you go, 2dc in the next stitch, [2dc, 2ch, 2dc] in the 2chsp, 2dc in the next stitch. Break black, leaving a 15cm tail. Switch to MC, 6dc. Do not join. Do not turn. (81) sts.

Round 7: (Always carry the MC under your other colours as you work around and only break the CC where indicated.) Continuing with MC, 1dc, switch to white, [1dc, (1htr, 1tr, 1htr) in the next stitch] five times, 1dc. Break white yarn, switch to MC, 7dc, switch to black, 2htr, 1dc, (2dc, 2ch, 2dc) in the 3chsp, 1dc, 2htr. Break black yarn, switch to MC, 13dc. Switch to black, 2htr, 1dc, (2dc, 2ch, 2dc) in the 3chsp, 1dc, 2htr. Break black yarn, switch to MC, 7dc. Switch to white, [1dc, (1htr, 1tr, 1htr) in the next stitch] five times, 1dc. Break white yarn, switch to MC, 1dc. Break yarn and weave in ends. (91) sts.

Body

Using MC, make 18ch.

Row 1: Starting in the 3rd chain from the hook (tch counts as 1htr), [(1dc, 1htr, 1tr) in the next stitch, miss 2] five times, 1htr. (17) sts.

Rows 2–76 (82, 90): 2ch (counts as htr), [(1dc, 1htr, 1tr) in tr, miss 2] five times, 1htr into the tch. (17) sts.
You will carry the MC underneath the white, but drop the white when not in use.

Rows 77 (83, 91) – 78 (84, 92): With MC, 2ch (counts as htr), [(1dc, 1htr, 1tr) in tr, miss 2] twice. Switch to white, (1dc, 1htr, 1tr) in tr, miss 2. Drop the white, switch to MC, [(1dc, 1htr, 1tr) in tr, miss 2] twice, 1htr.

Rows 79 (85, 93) – 80 (86, 94): With MC, 2ch, (1dc, 1htr, 1tr) in tr, miss 2. Switch to white, [(1dc, 1htr, 1tr) in tr, miss 2] three times. Drop the white, switch to MC, (1dc, 1htr, 1tr) in tr, miss 2, 1htr. Break MC.

Rows 81 (87, 95) – 88 (94, 102): In white, 2ch, [(1dc, 1htr, 1tr) in tr, miss 2] five times, 1htr. Turn.

Row 89 (95, 103): 3slst, [(1dc, 1htr, 1tr) in tr, miss 2] three times, 1slst. Turn. (12) sts.

Rows 90 (96, 104) – 92 (98, 106): [(1dc, 1htr, 1tr) in tr, miss 2] three times, 1slst. Turn.

Row 93 (99, 107): 4slst, (1dc, 1htr, 1tr) in tr, miss 2, slst. Turn. (3) sts.

Rows 94 (100, 108) – 95 (101, 109): (1dc, 1htr, 1tr) in tr, miss 2, slst. Break yarn and weave in ends.

Back Legs (Make 2)

Using black yarn, make 5ch.

Row 1: Starting from 2nd chain from hook, 4dc. (4)dc.

Rows 2–12: 1ch, 4dc. Turn. (4)dc. Break yarn, leaving a 15cm tail for sewing up.

Front Legs (Make 2)

Using MC, make 5ch.

Row 1: Starting from 2nd chain from hook, 4dc. (4)dc.

Rows 2–15: 1ch, 4dc. Turn. (4)dc.

Rows 16–19: In black, 1ch, 4dc. Turn. Break yarn, leaving a 15cm tail for sewing up.

Finishing

Using the tail left on the end of the nose, fold the nose in half, lengthways. Make a small stitch where the back meets the MC to keep the nose folded in half.

Use MC for all the sewing so it does not show through the front of the scarf. Using the photo for placement, place your fox face on top of the straight edge of the scarf, lining up the scarf edge with the top of the white whiskers on the face. Make sure the head is centred on the scarf. Sew the face securely to the body at the scarf edge and add a few tacking stitches at the fox forehead and ears to keep secure.

Sew the front legs onto the back of the face, just below the line of the scarf. They should come out at a 45-degree angle from the head.

Sew the back legs on, approximately 5cm up from the first row of white, again at a 45-degree angle to the body. Sew on the buttons for eyes, using the photograph for placement.

LEAFY CAPELET

Perfect for a walk in the woods to look for butterflies.

skill level: intermediate

Size	0-12 months	1 year	2 years	4 years	6 years
Finished length: bottom edge	92cm	96.5cm	102cm	107cm	112cm
Finished length: shoulder to hem	29cm	32cm	34cm	37cm	39.5cm
Yarn amounts	338m	402m	465m	549m	625m

MATERIALS:

- 3 (3,3,4,4) x 100g balls of Rowan Pure Wool Aran (100 per cent superwash wool), 186m Forest (676)
- 5mm/H8 hook
- 2 x buttons (1cm diameter)
- Tapestry needle

YARN REVIEW:

This lovely Aran-weight superwash wool is even softer and more wearable after it has been blocked.

YARN ALTERNATIVES:

Debbie Bliss Donegal Luxury Tweed Aran
Sublime Cashmere Merino Silk Aran

TENSION:

Work 12 sts and eight rows in HerrTr (see special stitches) to measure 10cm square using 5mm hook, or size required to obtain tension.

SPECIAL STITCHES:

Leaf

4ch, tr3tog into the base of the chain.

Treble 3 Together (tr3tog)

[YO, insert hook into stitch, YO, pull through stitch (three loops on hook), YO, pull through two loops] into three stitches. YO and pull through three loops. YO, pull through two remaining loops.

Herringbone Treble Crochet (HerrTr)

YO, insert hook into the stitch, YO, pull through stitch and first loop on hook, YO, pull through one loop, YO, pull through remaining two loops.

Herringbone Decrease (HerrTr2Tog)

YO, insert hook into the stitch, YO, pull through stitch and first loop on hook,

insert hook into the next stitch, YO, pull through stitch and first loop on hook, YO, pull through two loops, YO, pull through remaining two loops.

Crab Stitch (crab)

(Also known as reverse dc.) Worked in the opposite direction to a normal dc (working from left to right). Insert your hook from front to back into the next stitch to your right, YO, pull through stitch, YO, and pull through both loops on hook.

Pattern Notes:

• The cape is constructed from the bottom up, with the leaf edging made first.

• Stitches are then picked up along the long edge and a series of decreases are made up to the neck, where the hood is worked from the neck up.

• Count the chain stitches at the beginning of the row as a stitch.

INSTRUCTIONS

Leaf Border

Make 16 ch.

Row 1 (WS): 1ttr into 5th ch from hook (chain counts as 1ttr), make 1 leaf, miss 4, 1dc, make 1 leaf, miss 4, 2ttr. (4ttr, 1dc, 2 leaves).

Rows 2–35 (37, 39, 41, 45): 4ch, 1ttr, make 1 leaf, miss leaf, 1ttr, make 1 leaf, miss leaf, 2ttr. Turn. (5ttr, 2 leaves).

Row 36 (38, 40, 42, 46): 1ch (counts as 1dc), 1dc, 4ch, miss leaf, dc into the ttr between the 2 leaves, 4ch, miss leaf, 2dc. Turn. (5dc, 2 leaves).

With the yarn still connected, turn your work, WS facing, so you can work across the long edge of the leaf border.

Main Cape

Make 2ch (counts as 1dc and 1ch).

Row 1 (RS): (this row is worked into the end of each row of the leaf border) [3dc, 1ch] into the end of each row 36 (38, 40, 42, 44) times, 1dc into the beginning ch of the leaf border. Turn. 110 (116, 122, 128, 134)dc.

Rows 1–5 (7, 9, 11, 13): 3ch, work 1HerrTr into each dc across. Turn. 110 (116, 122, 128, 134)HerrTr.

Row 6 (8, 10, 12, 14): 3ch, [4HerrTr, HerrTr2tog] 18 (19, 20, 21, 22) times, 1HerrTr. Turn. 92 (97, 102, 107, 112) HerrTr.

Rows 7 (9, 11, 13, 15) – 9 (11, 13, 15, 17): 3ch, 91 (96, 101, 106, 111)HerrTr. Turn.

Row 10 (12, 14, 16, 18): 3ch, [3HerrTr, HerrTr2tog] 18 (19, 20, 21, 22) times, 1HerrTr. Turn. 74 (78, 82, 86, 90)HerrTr.

Row 11 (13, 15, 17, 19): 3ch, 73 (77, 81, 85, 89)HerrTr. Turn.

Row 12 (14, 16, 18, 20): 3ch, [2HerrTr, HerrTr2Tog] 18 (19, 20, 21, 22) times, 1HerrTr. Turn. 56 (59, 62, 65, 68)HerrTr.

Row 13 (15, 17, 19, 21): 3ch, 55 (58, 61, 64, 67)HerrTr. Turn.

Row 14 (16, 18, 20, 22): 3ch, 2(3, 0, 0, 2)HerrTr, [2(2, 3, 3, 3)HerrTr, HerrTr2tog] 12 times, 5 (7, 1, 4, 5) HerrTr. Turn. 44 (47, 50, 53, 56)HerrTr.

Hood

Row 1: 9 (8, 9, 8, 9)slst, 3ch, 25 (29, 31, 35, 37)HerrTr. Turn. 26 (30, 32, 36, 38) HerrTr.

Rows 2–6 (7, 8, 8, 9): 3ch, 25 (29, 31, 35, 37)HerrTr. Turn.

Row 7 (8, 9, 9, 10): 3ch, 2HerrTr in next, *1HerrTr, 2HerrTr in next; repeat from * across. 39 (45, 48, 54, 57)HerrTr.

Row 8 (9, 10, 10, 11): 3ch, HerrTr across. 39 (45, 48, 54, 57)HerrTr.

Row 9 (10, 11, 11, 12): 3ch, 0 (0, 0, 2, 3)HerrTr, [2HerrTr in next, 8 (20, 22, 7, 5)HerrTr] 4 (2, 2, 6, 8) times, 2HerrTr in next, 1 (1, 0, 2, 4)HerrTr. Turn. 44 (48, 51, 61, 66)HerrTr.

Rows 10 (11, 12, 12, 13) – 15 (17, 18, 20, 21): 3ch, HerrTr across. 44 (48, 51, 61, 66)HerrTr.

Finishing

Do not break yarn. Fold the last row in half, right sides together, stitches aligned. Working through two stitches at a time, slst the hood closed. Break yarn and weave in tails.

Edging

Turn the cape so it is upside down, right side facing. Attach the yarn so you can work across the edge of the leaf border first.

Round 1:

Work around the edge of the cape as follows:

4dc into the ttr that make up the end of the rows for the leaf.

Work each corner of the front of the cape 2dc, 2ch, 2dc.

Dc loosely into the end of each row
up the front of the cape.

Make one button loop at the top of
the front flap, one stitch down from the
corner near the hood. Work as follows:
make 5ch and slst into the next to last
dc you just made (working backwards),
work 5dc into the chsp.

Continue working dc around the hood
and back down the other side, working
another buttonhole as above on the
opposite side of the front from the first.
Join with a slst. Do NOT turn.

Round 2:

Work crab stitch around. Do not work
crab into the buttonhole. Join. Break
yarn and weave in ends.

Sew the button onto the opposite side
of the cape from the buttonhole, in line
with the hood edge.

Block the finished object to open up
the leaf edge and help it lie flat.

SHAGGY LION

My daughter's first word was 'Roar!' yelled at the top of her voice to anyone who would listen. It was only fitting I designed her suitable attire for such an activity.

skill level: beginner

Size	Newborn	Baby	Toddler	4+ years
Circumference	30.5cm	37cm	43cm	49cm
Height	11.5cm	13cm	16cm	19cm
Yarn amounts	49m	74m	92m	112m

MATERIALS:
- Main Colour (MC): 1 x 100g ball Rowan Cocoon (80 per cent merino wool, 20 per cent mohair), 115m/126y, Amber (215)
- Contrast Colour (CC): 1 x 100g ball of Patons Shadow Tweed (56 per cent wool, 40 per cent acrylic, 4 per cent viscose), Red, Burgundy, Orange (6906)
- 5.5mm/I9 hook
- Tapestry needle

YARN REVIEW:
A luxurious mix of wool and mohair, Rowan Cocoon is wonderful to work with. Combined with the wool for the mane this makes a very warm hat.

YARN ALTERNATIVES:
Wendy Mode Chunky
Twilleys Freedom

TENSION:
Work 13 stitches and 9.5 rounds in half treble crochet to measure 10cm square using a 5.5mm hook, or size required to obtain tension.

PATTERN NOTES:
- The hat is worked in the round until mid-forehead to keep the mane out of the face and eyes of the wearer.
- Switching then to rows, the back and sides of the hat are built up with stitches decreased in the very last row at the back to keep the bottom tucked in nicely.
- Earflaps are then built up on either side. The mane is tied on strand by strand.
- When working in the round on the top portion of the hat, do not count the chain 2 as a stitch. When you switch to rows, it will be added to your overall stitch count.

INSTRUCTIONS:

Turn your work at the end of each round.

Using MC, 2ch and make 8htr into a magic loop. Join. (8)htr.

Round 1: 2ch. *2htr into each stitch; repeat from * around. Join. (16)htr.

Round 2: 2ch, *1htr, 2htr into the next; repeat from * around. Join. (24)htr.

Round 3: 2ch, *2htr, 2htr into the next; repeat from * around. Join. (32)htr.

Round 4: 2ch, *3htr, 2htr into next; repeat from * around. Join. (40)htr.

For Newborn size, continue to Round 8.

Round 5: 2ch, *4htr, 2htr into next; repeat from * around. Join. (48)htr.

For Baby size, continue to Round 8.

Round 6: 2ch, *5htr, 2htr into next; repeat from * around. Join. (56)htr.

For Toddler size, continue to Round 8.

Round 7: 2ch, *6htr, 2htr into next; repeat from * around. Join. (64)htr.

Rounds 8–9 (11, 13, 15): work even for 2 (4, 6, 8) rounds.

Back of Hat

Rows 1–3 (4, 4, 4): 2ch, 31 (35, 41, 47) htr. Turn. 32 (36, 42, 48)htr.

Row 4 (5, 5, 5): 2ch, 12 (13, 15, 17)htr, htr2tog, 2 (4, 6, 8)htr, htr2tog, 13 (14, 16, 18)htr. Turn. 30 (34, 40, 46)htr.

Earflaps

Row 1: 2ch, 9 (11, 13, 15)htr. Turn. 10 (12, 14, 16)htr.

Row 2: 2ch, 1htr, htr2tog, htr to end. Turn. 9 (11, 13, 15)htr.

Row 3 – (4, 6, 8, 10): repeat row 2 until 7 sts remain.

Break yarn, leaving a 25cm tail.

Rejoin yarn at the first stitch of the last built up row at the front of the hat on the other side. Repeat the earflap from row 1.

Finishing

Edging

Starting in the bottom of one of the earflaps, right side facing, make 1ch and dc around the edges of the earflaps and hat to ensure a nice even finish to the hat. This can be done in the wool for the mane or the hat.

Earflap Plait (Make 2)

Earflap plaits are made using six 30cm lengths of yarn (MC and/or CC).

Weave your tails from the earflaps through to the central space between the stitches at the bottom of your earflap.

Thread the lengths of additional wool through the same spaces.

Fold in half.

Using one length of wool, wrap around all of the tails and tie tightly, ensuring the wrapping strand is tucked under the wrap.

Braid to desired length.

Wrap and tie as above.

Trim as required.

Mane

Using CC, cut lengths of wool approximately 12.5cm in length.

Top Tip: To cut a lot of strips at once, wrap the yarn multiple numbers of times around your non-dominant hand. Cut through the top and bottom loops. Thread your hook through the spaces between the stitches. Fold length of mane in half and use your hook to pull through the gap in the stitches. Catch both cut ends in your hook and pull through the loop on your hook. Pull ends tightly to secure to hat. You'll need an approximately 1.5cm wide strip of mane around the front of the face (slightly more on the top). Do not tie mane directly around the edging as you do not want fluff getting into your wearer's face.

Ears

Using MC, make 2ch, and 8htr into a magic loop. Join.

Round 2: 2ch, *2htr in each stitch; repeat from * around. Join and break yarn. (16)htr.

(If the ears cannot be seen over the mane at this stage – add Round 3: 2ch, *htr1, 2htr in next; repeat from * around. Join and break yarn.)

Using the photos for placement, sew ears onto hat. Weave in ends.

MANY-WAYS ALICE BANDS

Who doesn't have 101 scraps of yarn lying around? These little projects only take small amounts of wool and are quickly attached to store-bought alice bands for a fun accessory or quick costume. In addition to the bow and the butterfly, you can also use the ear patterns from the Shaggy Lion hat and the Wolf jacket.

skill level: beginner

Type	Bow	Butterflies	Wolf Ears	Lion Ears
Width	10cm	5cm	5cm	7.5cm
Yarn amounts	26m	9m	11m	8m

MATERIALS:

For Bow
- 26m of any DK-weight yarn. Sample made in: Sirdar Snuggly Baby Bamboo DK (80 per cent bamboo, 20 per cent wool), 95m Coo (148)
- 3.75mm/F5 hook

For Butterflies
- 9m of any DK-weight yarn. Sample made in: Sirdar Snuggly Baby Bamboo DK (80 per cent bamboo, 20 per cent wool), 95m Cream (131)
- 3.75mm/F5 hook

For Circular Ears
- 8m of any bulky weight yarn. Sample made in: Wendy Mode Chunky (50 per cent wool, 50 per cent acrylic), 140m Coffee Bean (218)
- Pipe cleaner or florist's wire
- 6mm/J10 hook

For Triangular Ears
- ◎ 11m of any DK-weight yarn. Sample made in Wendy Mode DK (50 per cent wool, 50 per cent acrylic), 142m Fog (232)
- ◎ Pipe cleaner or florist's wire
- ◎ 4mm/G6 hook

All
- ◎ 1 x headband (instructions included for both moulded plastic and elastic varieties)
- ◎ Tapestry needle
- ◎ Hot glue (optional)

TENSION:
Tension is not critical to this project – a larger hook and wool will make a larger accessory.

PATTERN NOTES:
In addition to these projects, you can also use the ears from the Wolf Jacket and the Shaggy Lion hat. Go to the 'Finishing' section for instructions on securing the ears to either a structured headband or a soft elastic one.

INSTRUCTIONS:
Sweet Bumpy Bow

With 3.75mm hook and yarn for the bow, make 39ch. Join in the round.

Round 1: 1ch (does not count as a stitch), working into the back bumps of the chain, 39dc. Turn. (39)dd.

Round 2: 1ch (does not count as a stitch), 1dc, ★1dc, 1dtr repeat from ★ around. Turn.

Round 3: 1ch, 39dc. Turn.

Rounds 4–9: repeat rounds 2–3. Break yarn and weave in ends.

Finishing
Fold the tube in half so that the seam is at the back of your work. Gather the bow together at the middle and tie one end of yarn securely around the centre to keep it gathered, leaving a 7.5cm tail hanging. Wrap repeatedly, until the central wrap is approximately 2.5cm in width. Cut the yarn and tie the newly cut end to the beginning tail. Use your crochet hook to hide ends inside the wrap.

Butterfly
Large

Using 3.75mm hook and yarn for the butterfly, 1ch (does not count as a stitch), [1dc, 2ch] four times into a magic loop. Join. (4)dc.

Round 1: 1ch, miss 1, 6dtr into 2chsp, 1slst, [6htr into 2chsp, 1slst] twice, 6dtr into 2chsp. Join. Break yarn, leaving a 4cm tail for sewing. (24)dc.

Small

With 3.75mm hook and yarn for the butterfly, 1ch (does not count as a stitch), [1dc, 2ch] four times into a magic loop. Join. (4dc).

Round 1: 1ch, miss 1, 6htr into 2chsp, 1slst, [6dc into 2chsp, 1slst] twice, 6htr into 2chsp. Join. Break yarn, leaving a 4cm tail for sewing. (24).

Abdomen
Cut a length of yarn for butterfly approximately 15cm in length. Leaving a 5cm tail at the top, wrap the yarn around the width of the butterfly three times and tie off the ends. Make a small knot at the ends of the tails to form the balls on top of the antennae and trim to size.

Finishing
Moulded Plastic Alice Band

To secure the details on the moulded plastic band, thread a tapestry needle with matching yarn.

For the Flower/Butterfly: Position the item over a place where there are teeth in the headband on the opposite side. Work the needle through the back side of the wrapped yarn and into the underside of the item and down out again, making sure the needle does not come through the front side of the item. Wrap yarn around the plastic of the headband. Make several secure loops like this through the item and around the headband. Tie off. Using your crochet hook, pull the loose ends into the wrapped yarn. A dot of hot glue will help them stay in place.

Elastic Headband
To secure the details on the elastic band, thread a tapestry needle with matching yarn. (It may help to use a slightly sharper needle. If your yarn is too thick to be threaded through the eye, split the yarn ply apart or use matching thread or embroidery floss.)

For the Flower/Butterfly: Position item, work the needle through the back side of the wrapped yarn and into the underside of the item and down out again, making sure the needle does not come through the front side of the item. Then push needle through the elastic of the headband. Make several secure loops like this through the item and headband. Tie off. Using your crochet hook, pull the loose ends into the wrapped yarn. A dot of hot glue will help them stay in place.

Triangular Ears

Follow the pattern for the ears of the Wolf on page 113, up until the point of holding 2 together to join. Shape a small piece of pipe cleaner or florist's wire into a triangle, just smaller than ears. Place inside and dc around as indicated in the pattern.

Circular Ears

Follow the pattern for the ears of the Shaggy Lion on page 42, up until the point of holding two together to join. Shape a small piece of pipe cleaner or florist's wire into a circle, just smaller than ears. Place inside and dc around as indicated in the pattern.

Finishing
Moulded Plastic Alice Band

To secure the details on the moulded plastic band, thread a tapestry needle with matching yarn.

For the Ears: Position ears over a place where there are teeth in the headband

on the opposite side. Push needle through the bottom of the ears, over the pipe cleaner and through the other side (the pipe cleaner should be between the sewing yarn and the headband) and then down around the plastic of the headband. Make several secure loops through the ears and around the headband. Tie off. Repeat for second ear. Using your crochet hook, pull the loose ends into the middle of the ear 'sandwich'. A dot of hot glue will help them stay in place.

Elastic Headband

To secure the details on the elastic band, thread a tapestry needle with matching yarn. (It may help to use a slightly sharper needle. If your yarn is too thick to be threaded through the eye, split the yarn ply apart or use matching thread or embroidery floss.)

For the Ears: Position ears, push needle through the bottom of the ears, over the pipe cleaner and through the other side (the pipe cleaner should be between the sewing yarn and the headband) and then down into the elastic of the headband. Make several secure loops through the ears, over the wire and around and through the headband. Tie off. Repeat for second ear. Using your crochet hook, pull the loose ends into the middle of the ear 'sandwich'. A dot of hot glue will help them stay in place.

WITCH / WIZARD / PRINCESS

Floppy, warm and made with Super Chunky wool your little magical creatures will be off making magic in no time.

skill level: beginner

Size	Newborn	Baby	Toddler	4+ years
Finished circumference	36cm	40cm	44cm	52cm
Finished height	20cm	25.5cm	28cm	32cm
Yarn amounts Wizard/Princess	29m	35.8m	43.6m	61.5m
Yarn amounts Witch	52m	64m	96m	116m

MATERIALS:

For Wizard
- 1 x 150g hank Malabrigo Rasta (100 per cent merino wool), 82m Azules (856)

For Witch
- 1 (1, 2, 2) x 150g hank Malabrigo Rasta (100 per cent merino wool), 82m Black (195)

For Princess
- 2 (2, 3, 4) x 50g balls Sirdar Big Softie Super Chunky (51 per cent wool, 49 per cent acrylic), 45m Pink (347)
- 6.5mm/K10.5 hook
- Tapestry needle
- Stitch marker

YARN REVIEW:
This partially felted, Super Chunky wool works up quickly.

YARN ALTERNATIVES:
Seriously Chunky by Cygnet
Serenity Super Chunky by Wendy

TENSION:
Work 7.5 sts and 8 rounds in double

Pattern notes: This pattern is worked entirely in the round in the amigurumi style, with no seams or turning chains at the start of the rounds.
Use a stitch marker to mark the beginning of the round. Do not turn your work at the end of the rounds.

crochet to measure 10cm square using 6.5mm hook, or size required to obtain tension.

INSTRUCTIONS:
1ch, 4dc into a magic loop. (4)dc.
Round 1: *1dc, 2dc into dc; repeat from * around. (6)dc.
Round 2: 6dc.
Round 3: *1dc, 2dc into dc; repeat from * around. (9)dc.
Round 4: 9dc.
Round 5: *2dc, 2dc into dc; repeat from * around. (12)dc.
Round 6: 12dc.
Round 7: *3dc, 2dc into dc; repeat from * around. (15)dc.
Round 8: 15dc.
Round 9: *4dc, 2dc into dc; repeat from * around. (18)dc.
Round 10: 18dc.
Round 11: *5dc, 2dc into dc; repeat from * around. (21)dc.
Round 12: 21dc.
Round 13: *6dc, 2dc into dc; repeat from * around. (24)dc.
Round 14: 24dc.

Round 15: *7dc, 2dc into dc; repeat from * around. (27)dc.
Round 16: 27dc.

For sizes Baby, Toddler and 4+ years ONLY
Round 17: *8dc, 2dc into dc; repeat from * around. (30)dc.
Round 18: 30dc.

For sizes Toddler and 4+ years ONLY
Round 19: *9dc, 2dc into dc; repeat from * around. (33)dc.
Round 20: 33dc.

For size 4+ years ONLY
Round 21: *10dc, 2dc into dc* repeat from * around (36)dc.
Round 22: 36dc.
Round 23: *11dc, 2dc into dc; repeat from * around (39)dc.
Round 24: 39dc.

For ALL sizes
Work 4 (4, 5, 6) rows even. Finish off

for the Wizard and Princess variations, or continue to Brim section for Witch variation.
Brim for Witch's Hat
Round 1: (working into FLO) *2dc, 2dc in dc; repeat from * around. 36 (40, 44, 52)dc.
Round 2: *3dc, 2dc in dc; repeat from * around. 45 (50, 55, 65)dc.
Round 3: *4dc, 2dc in dc; repeat from * around. 54 (60, 66, 78)dc.
Round 4: *5dc, 2dc in dc; repeat from * around. 63 (70, 77, 91)dc.

For sizes Newborn and Baby ONLY
Break yarn and weave in ends.

For sizes Toddler and 4+ years ONLY
Round 5: 2dc in dc stitch, - (-, 42, 44)dc, 2dc in dc stitch, dc to end (88, 104).
Round 6: 2dc in dc stitch, - (-, 43, 45)dc, 2dc in dc stitch, dc to end (99, 117).
Break yarn and weave in ends.

WRAP AROUND

A sweet little shawl, perfect for dressing up or keeping warm, or both.

skill level: beginner

Size	0-12 months	1 year	2 years	4 years	6 years
Finished length	71cm	85cm	91cm	103cm	111cm
Yarn amounts	99m	141m	163m	185m	213m

MATERIALS:
- 1 (2, 2, 2, 2) x 50g ball of Sublime Baby Cashmere Merino Silk DK (75 per cent extra fine merino, 20 per cent silk, 5 per cent cashmere), 116m Pebble (006)
- 4mm/G6 hook
- 2 x buttons (7.5–10cm diameter)
- Tapestry needle

YARN REVIEW:
The drape and softness of this DK-weight silk-blend yarn is simple, yet gorgeous.

YARN ALTERNATIVES:
Debbie Bliss Cashmerino DK
Rowan Cashsoft DK

TENSION:
Work 18 sts and seven rows in treble crochet to measure 10cm square using 4mm hook, or size required to obtain tension.

SPECIAL STITCHES:
Puff Stitch (PS)
[YO, insert hook into stitch and draw up a loop] three times (seven loops on hook). YO and pull through six loops on hook. YO and pull through last two loops on hook.

Pattern notes: This shawl is constructed from side to side. Increases are only worked on the side next to the cable and puff pattern, giving it a long, shallow shape.

INSTRUCTIONS:

Count the 3ch at the beginning of each row as a stitch.

Make 9ch.

Row 1 (RS): Starting in the 4th ch from hook (counts as 1tr), 2tr, miss 1ch, [1PS, 1ch, 1PS] into the next ch, miss 1ch, 1tr. Turn. 6sts.

Row 2: 3ch, [1PS, 1ch, 1PS] into the chsp in between the 2 PS, 1RdtrB into the next tr, 2tr into tr, 1tr into the tch. Turn. 7sts.

Row 3: 3ch, 1tr, 2tr in tr, 1RdtrF, [1PS, 1ch, 1PS] into the chsp in between the 2 PS, RdtrF around the tch. 8sts.

Row 4: 3ch, [1PS, ch, 1PS] into the chsp in between the 2 PS, 1RdtrB, 2tr into tr, 3tr. Turn. 9sts.

Repeat rows 3–4 8 (10, 11, 12, 13) times until you have 25 (29, 31, 33, 35) stitches.

Rows 21 (25, 27, 29, 31) – 29 (35, 37, 43, 47): Work even.

Decreasing

Row 1: 3ch, 18 (21, 24, 26, 28)tr, tr2tog, RdtrF, [1PS, 1ch, 1PS] into the chsp in between the 2PS, RdtrF around the tch. 24 (28, 30, 32, 34) sts.

Row 2: 3ch, [1PS, 1ch, 1PS] into the chsp in between the 2 PS, RdtrB, tr2tog, 18 (21, 24, 26, 28)tr. Turn. 23 (27, 29, 31, 33) sts.

Repeat rows 1–2 8 (10, 11, 12, 13) times.

Work row 1 once. (6 sts remain.)

Cut yarn and weave in ends.

Edging

With RS facing, join the yarn on the short edge of the wrap.

1ch, 4dc, turn, 4ch, slst into the 2nd dc made, turn, 5dc into the loop, continue working into the short edge 1dc, [1dc, 2ch, 1dc] into the corner stitch, continue to dc along the long straight edge [1dc, 2ch, 1dc] into the corner stitch, 4dc, turn, 4ch, slst into the 2nd dc made, turn, 5dc into the loop, 2dc into the short edge. Break yarn and weave in ends.

Using your child as a guide for their placement, sew buttons onto the back of shawl, on the inside, in line with the edging.

FINGERS, KNEES AND TOES

Baby Ballet Slippers
Beastie Feet
Sunshine and Showers Mittens
Glass Slippers
Hedgehog Mittens
Leg Warmers
Mermaid Tail
Tutu

BABY BALLET SLIPPERS

Delicate little ballet slippers for delicate baby feet.

skill level: intermediate

Size	Extra small	Medium	Large	Extra large
Foot width	5cm	6cm	6cm	6.5cm
Foot length	9cm	10cm	11cm	12.5cm
Yarn amounts	33m	41m	47m	58m

MATERIALS:
- 1 x 50g ball of Sirdar Snuggly Baby Bamboo DK (80 per cent bamboo, 20 per cent wool), 95m Flip Flop (125)
- 4mm/G6 hook
- 19 (20, 21, 24)cm of thin elastic cord or doubled shirring elastic tied or sewn into a loop
- 17.5cm ribbon for ties
- Embroidery needle

YARN REVIEW:
Silky and drapey, this is a fabulous yarn to add a bit of sheen to your slippers.

YARN ALTERNATIVES:
Sublime Cashmere Merino Silk DK

TENSION:
Work 17 sts and 23 rows in double crochet to measure 10cm square using 4mm hook, or size required to obtain tension.

NOTE ON SIZING:
These are sized up to approximately age two.

Pattern note: Turn your work at the end of each round.

INSTRUCTIONS:

Toe

1ch, 4dc into a magic loop. Join. Turn. (4)dc.

Round 1: 1ch (does not count as a stitch), 2dc into each stitch around. Join. (8)dc.

Round 2: 1ch, ★1dc, 2dc into dc; repeat from ★ to end. Join. (12)dc.

Round 3: 1ch, ★2dc, 2dc into dc; repeat from ★ to end. Join. (16)dc.

Round 4: 1ch, ★3dc, 2dc into dc; repeat from ★ to end. Join. (20)dc.

For sizes Medium, Large, and Extra large ONLY

Round 5: 1ch, ★4dc, 2dc into dc; repeat from ★ to end. Join. - (24, 24, 24)dc.

For size Extra large ONLY

Round 6: 1ch, ★5dc, 2dc into dc; repeat from ★ to end. Join. - (-, -, 28).

For ALL sizes

Work even for 2 (3, 3, 3) rounds.

Sole

Set-up: 7 (9, 9, 11)slst. Turn to move the line of joined stitches to the bottom of the sole.

Rows 1–13 (15, 16, 18): With WS (RS, WS, RS) facing 1ch, 15 (19, 19, 22)dc. Turn. 15 (19, 19, 22)dc.

Fold the last row in half, right sides together, lining up the stitches; slst through all four loops along. Break yarn and weave in ends.

Edging

You are going to work around the elastic as you dc the edging. This will help the slipper stay on.

Round 1: Re-attach yarn at the top of the slipper, at the back where the slst seam is. Working around the elastic, 1ch, 31 (35, 39, 44)dc, 6ch, 1dc into the same stitch to form a loop. Break yarn and weave in ends.

Finishing

Thread the length of ribbon through the loop at the back.

BEASTIE FEET

Fact: Slippers with claws are a childhood requirement.

skill level: intermediate

Size	0–6 months	6–12 months	1 year	2 years	4 years	6 years
Foot width	5cm	5.5cm	5.5cm	6cm	6.5cm	6.5cm
Foot length	9cm	10cm	11cm	12.5cm	16cm	16.5cm
Yarn amounts	27m	34m	37m	45m	57m	70m

MATERIALS:
- Main Colour (MC): 1 x 250g ball of Cascade Eco+ (100 per cent Peruvian wool), 250m Night Vision (8025)
- Contrast Colour (CC): Small amount of Cascade 220 (100 per cent Peruvian wool), Black (8555)
- 4mm/G6 hook
- 6mm/J10 hook
- 6.5mm/K10.5 hook
- 12.5 (14, 15, 15, 16, 17.5)cm of 0.75cm wide elastic webbing
- Tapestry needle

YARN REVIEW:
Excellent value for money, one hank of this tweedy, chunky-weight yarn will make slippers for the whole family.

YARN ALTERNATIVES:
Wendy Mode Chunky

TENSION:
Work 15 sts and eight rounds in half treble crochet to measure 10cm square using a 6mm hook, or size required to obtain tension.

SPECIAL STITCHES:
Slip Stitch Ribbing
Slst in BLO. This can be tricky to get to begin with, so just ensure you are crocheting loosely.

Pattern notes: Of all of the crochet slippers I have made and worn over the years, those with a double sole are by far the most comfortable and worth the extra effort. The crochet soles are made first, then attached in pairs. The heel is worked directly onto the soles, then the top of the slipper is constructed separately then sewn on.
Chain stitches at the beginning of the rows and rounds.
Do not count, unless otherwise stated.

INSTRUCTIONS:

Soles (Make 4)

Using the middle-sized hook and MC, make 7 (9, 10, 11, 13, 15) chain.

Round 1: 2htr in the 3rd chain from hook, 3 (5, 6, 7, 9, 11)htr, 7 (8, 7, 7, 7, 8) htr in the last stitch, turning your work as you go to work into the other side of chain, 3 (5, 6, 7, 9, 11)htr, 2htr in the last stitch (this is the same stitch that you made 2htr into at the beginning of the round). Join. Do not turn. 17 (22, 23, 25, 29, 34)htr.

For sizes 0–6 months and 6–12 months ONLY

Round 2: 1ch, [2dc in htr] twice, 3 (5, -, -, -, -)dc, [2dc in htr] seven(eight, -, -, -, -) times, 3 (5, -, -, -, -)dc, [2dc in htr] twice. Join. Do not turn. 28, (34, -, -, -, -)dc.

For sizes 1 year, 2 years, 4 years and 6 years ONLY

Round 2: 1ch, [2dc in htr] twice, -(-, 3, 4, 5, 6)dc, - (-, 3, 3, 4, 5)htr, [2dc in htr] - (-, eight, seven, seven, eight) times, - (-, 3, 3, 4, 5)htr, - (-, 3, 4, 5, 6)dc, [2dc in htr] twice. Join. Do not turn. - (-, 34, 36, 40, 46) sts.

For ALL sizes

Round 3: 1ch, 3dc, 2dc in dc, 3 (5, 6, 7, 9, 11)dc, [2dc in next stitch, 1dc] 7 (8, 7, 7, 7, 8) times, 3 (5, 6, 7, 9, 11)dc, 2dc in dc, 3dc. Join. Do not turn. 37 (44, 43, 45, 49, 56)dc.

Hold two soles wrong sides together and slst together through the BLO (these are the two inner loops in the 'sandwich'). Cut the yarn and weave in the ends.

Heels

Row 1: Find the central backstitch of the soles (the one where the slst joined the last round of the sole). Count 8 (9, 9, 9, 11, 11) stitches towards the toe. Working into the unworked loop of the top sole inside facing, 1ch, 17 (19, 19, 19, 23, 23)dc towards the centre back. Turn. 17 (19, 19, 19, 23, 23)dc.

Row 2: 1ch, 17 (19, 19, 19, 23, 23)dc. Turn. 17 (19, 19, 19, 23, 23)dc.

Work 0 (0, 0, 1, 2, 4) rows even.

Row 3 (3, 3, 4, 5, 7): 1ch, 2dc, dc2tog, 9 (11, 11, 11, 15, 15)dc, dc2tog, 2dc. Turn. 15 (17, 17, 17, 21, 21)dc.

Row 4 (4, 4, 5, 6, 8): (Tie or sew the elastic in a loop. You will work around the elastic for this last round.) 1ch, 15 (17, 17, 17, 21, 21)dc. Break yarn and weave in ends. 15 (17, 17, 17, 21, 21)dc.

Front Uppers (Make 2)

Using the largest hook and MC, make 9 (11, 12, 13, 15, 16)ch.

Row 1 (RS): (working in the back bumps of the chain) starting in 2nd chain from hook, 8 (10, 11, 13, 14, 15)slst. Turn. 8 (10, 11, 13, 14, 15)slst.

Row 2: 1ch, 8 (10, 11, 13, 14, 15)slst BLO. Turn. 8 (10, 11, 13, 14, 15)slst.

Row 3: 2ch. Starting in the 2nd ch from hook, 9 (11, 12, 13, 15, 16)slst BLO. Turn. 9 (11, 12, 13, 15, 16)slst.

Rows 4–10 (14, 14, 18, 20, 24): 1ch, 9 (11, 12, 13, 15, 16)slst BLO. Turn. 9 (11, 12, 13, 15, 16)slst.

Row 11 (15, 15, 19, 21, 25): 1ch, 8 (10, 11, 13, 14, 15)slst BLO. Miss 1. Turn. 8 (10, 11, 13, 14, 15)slst.

Row 12 (16, 16, 20, 22, 26): 1ch, 8 (10, 11, 13, 14, 15)slst BLO. Turn.

Edging and Sewing on Upper

Row 1 (WS): Using the smallest hook, dc around 3 edges of the upper (not the top, straight edge), as follows:

Working down the sides, work through both loops of the slst ribbing.

Working the curved bottom edge, dc in every other row.

22 (28, 30, 36, 39, 43)dc.

Turn.

Row 2 (RS): Place upper on top of toe end of slipper, RS up. Line up the curved edge with the toe of the soles. Overlap the straight edge of the upper with the front side of the heel by 2 (3, 4, 5, 5, 6) stitches. Sew the upper onto the soles of the shoe, working around the posts of the dc edging and through both layers of sole. (You can also slst the uppers in place, using the unworked loop on the upper sole.) To keep the top straight, it may help to pin it in place as you work.

Row 3: Re-attach yarn to work across the straight edge of upper. Working into every other row, 2 (3, 3, 4, 4, 5)dc, 2 (2, 2, 2, 3, 3)dc working around the elastic that remains uncovered from the heel section, 2 (3, 3, 4, 4, 5)dc. Break yarn. 6 (8, 8, 10, 11, 13)dc.

Claws (Make 2)

Using the smallest hook and the yarn for the claws, [4ch, starting with the 2nd chain from hook, 1dc, 1htr, 1tr] four times. Lightly block or steam iron to help the claws lie flat. Sew onto the front of the slipper.

SUNSHINE AND SHOWERS MITTENS

Convertible mittens are just perfect for kids, with the flexibility to keep little fingers warm, but still allowing them to explore and play.

skill level: beginner

Size	Small	Medium	Large
Circumference	11.5cm	14cm	16.5cm
Length	11.5cm	14.5cm	17cm
Yarn amounts	66m	100m	137m

MATERIALS:
- Main Colour (MC): 1 x 100g hank of Cascade 220 (100 per cent Peruvian wool), 201m Silver Grey (8401)
- A small amount of Cascade 220 (100 per cent Peruvian wool), 201m in the following colours:
  - Cloud: Charcoal (8400)
  - Sun: Sunflower (2415)
  - Sun rays: Orange Sherbet (7825)
  - Rain: Blueberry (9464)
  - Rainbow: colours as above, plus:
    - Christmas Red (8895) and Christmas Green (8894)
- 4mm/G6 hook
- 4.5mm/7 hook
- 2 x buttons (1cm in diameter)
- Tapestry needle
- Stitch marker

YARN REVIEW:
Cascade 220 is a versatile worsted weight wool, comes in a huge range of colours and has excellent stitch definition.

YARN ALTERNATIVES:
Quince and Co. Lark

TENSION:
Work 15.5 sts and 18 rows in double crochet to measure 10cm square using a 4.5mm hook, or size required to obtain tension.

SPECIAL STITCHES:
Foundation Half Treble Crochet (fhtrc)
First stitch:
Make 2ch, YO hook, insert hook into the first chain, YO and pull through stitch (three loops on hook). This is the joining stitch. YO and pull through first loop on hook (three loops on hook). This is the 'chain' stitch. YO and pull through all three loops on hook.

Following Stitches:
YO hook, insert hook into the 'chain' from the previous stitch, YO and pull through stitch (three loops on hook). This is the joining stitch. YO and pull through first loop on hook (three loops on hook). This is the 'chain' stitch. YO and pull through all three loops on hook.

PATTERN NOTES:
- Do not count the chains at the beginning of the round as a stitch.
- Do not turn your work at the end of each round.

INSTRUCTIONS (Make 2, but follow the instructions for Left and Right Mitten)

Round 1: With smaller hook and MC, make 18 (22, 26)fhtrc. Join in the round. 18 (22, 26)fhtrc.

Rounds 2–4 (5, 6): 3ch, *RtrF, RtrB; repeat from * to end. Join.

Rounds 5 (6, 7) – 8 (10, 11): Switch to larger hook, 1ch, 18 (22, 26)dc. Join.

Thumbhole – Left Mitten
Round 9 (11, 12): 1ch (does not count as a stitch), 1dc, 3 (4, 5)ch, miss 3 (4, 5) stitches, 14 (17, 20)dc. Join into the first chain of the thumbhole at the beginning of the round. 15 (18, 21)dc.

Thumbhole – Right Mitten
Round 9 (11, 12): 1ch, 14 (17, 20)dc, 3 (4, 5)ch, miss 3 (4, 5) stitches, 1dc. Join. 15 (18, 21)dc.

Both Mittens
Round 10 (12, 13): 1ch, 18 (22, 26)dc, working into just one loop of the chain stitches when you come across them. Join. 18 (22, 26)dc.

Rounds 11 (13, 14) – 13 (16, 18): 1ch, 18 (22, 26)dc. Join.

Flap Set-up – Left Mitten
Round 14 (17, 19): 1ch, 4 (5 ,6)dc, 7 (9, 11)dc in BLO (it may be useful to mark the unworked loops with a stitch marker so you can find them easily again), 7 (8, 9)dc in both loops. Join. 18 (22, 26)dc.

Flap Set-up – Right Mitten
Round 14 (17, 19): 1ch, 7 (8, 9)dc, 7 (9, 11)dc in BLO (it may be useful to mark the unworked loops with a stitch marker so you can find them easily again), 4 (5, 6)dc in both loops. Join. 18 (22, 26)dc.

Both Mittens
Rounds 15 (18, 20) – 17 (20, 23): 1ch, 18 (22, 26)dc. Join. Break yarn.

Flap
Round 1: Join yarn to the first unworked loop of round 14 (17, 19) of the mitten, RS facing. 1ch, work 7 (9, 11)dc in free loops of the mitten, then 13 (15, 17)ch. Join to 1st dc of the round.

7 (9, 11)dc and 13 (15, 17)ch.

Rounds 2–3 (4, 6): 7 (9, 11)dc across the dc and 13 (15, 17)dc into the ch. Join. 20 (24, 27)dc.

Round 4 (5, 7): 1ch, [dc2tog] ten (twelve, fourteen) times. Join.10 (12, 14)dc.

Round 5 (6, 8): 1ch, 10 (12, 14)dc. Join.

Round 6 (7, 9): 1ch, [dc2tog] five (six, seven) times. Do not join. 5 (6, 7)dc.

Button Loop
Make 4 ch, miss 2 (3, 3)dc, 1slst. Break yarn and pull through, leaving a 15cm tail past the chain. Using a tapestry needle, sew the top of the mitten closed by weaving the yarn in and out of the last 5 (6, 7) stitches, pulling them tight to close, but leaving the 4ch loose at the top to act as a button loop. Tie off end.

Thumb

Round 1: Rejoin yarn at the missed stitches at the thumb opening, 1ch, 6 (8, 10)dc around, working into the missed stitches and the unworked side of the chain. Join. 6 (8, 10)dc.

Rounds 2–4 (5, 6): 1ch, 6 (8, 10)dc. Join.

Round 5 (6, 7): 1ch, [dc2tog] three (four, five) times. 3 (4, 5)dc. Break yarn, leaving a 15cm tail. Using a tapestry needle, sew the top of the mitten closed by weaving the yarn in and out of the last 3 (4, 5) stitches, pulling them tight to close. Tie off end.

Cloud (Makes 2)

Using yarn for the cloud and the smaller hook, make 4ch.

Round 1: 2dc into the 2nd chain from hook, 1dc, 4dc in the next ch, turning your work to work into other side of chain, 1dc, 2dc in the next ch. Join. (10)dc.

Round 2: 6tr into the same stitch, [1slst, 6tr into the next stitch] twice, 1slst. (21) sts.

Using the photo for placement, sew onto the back of each mitten.

Sun

Using yarn for the sun and smaller hook, 1ch (does not count as a stitch), 6dc into a magic loop. Join. (6)dc.

Round 1: 1ch (does not count as a stitch), [2dc in the next dc] six times. Join. (12)dc.

Fasten off and weave in ends.

Using the photo for placement, sew onto the hand side of the mitten flap using a backstitch around the edge of the circle.

Rainbow

Using the photos for placement, embroider a rainbow onto one side of the mitten flap.

Finishing

To add the lines of rain and sun rays, thread your needle with the appropriate wool and use the running stitch to sew lines coming down from the cloud and rays coming out from the sun.

Using your button loop as a guide, sew on the button to the back of the mitten to keep the flap up.

GLASS SLIPPERS

Lacy and delicate, these quick slippers add
a touch of glamour to any little feet.

skill level: intermediate

Size	0-6 months	6-12 months	1 year	2 years
Width	5cm	5.5cm	5.5cm	5.5cm
Length	9cm	10cm	11.5cm	13cm
Yarn amounts	37m	38.5m	52m	62m

MATERIALS:
- 1 x 50g skein of Malabrigo Silky Merino (51 per cent silk, 49 per cent merino wool), 138m Cape Cod Grey (429)
- 3.75mm/F5 hook
- 2 x buttons (1cm in diameter)
- Tapestry needle
- 19 (20, 21, 24)cm of thin elastic cord or doubled shirring elastic tied or sewn into a loop

YARN REVIEW:
Silky and soft, this glamorous DK yarn is a joy to work with.

YARN ALTERNATIVES:
Fyberspates Scrumptious Silk DK

TENSION:
Work 21sts and 23 rounds in single crochet to measure 10cm square using a 3.75mm hook, or size required to obtain gauge.

PATTERN NOTES:
- Do not count the 1ch at the beginning of the round as a stitch.
- Do not turn your work at the end of each round, unless indicated.

SPECIAL STITCHES:
Toe Gather
[YO twice, miss one, insert hook into next stitch, YO and pull through stitch, (YO and pull through two loops) twice] six times (seven loops on hook), YO, pull through all the loops on hook.

INSTRUCTIONS:
Make 12 (13, 15, 17)ch.

Round 1: 2dc in 2nd ch from hook, 9 (10, 12, 14)dc, 4dc in last stitch, turning as you go. Working in other side of the chain, 9 (10, 12, 14)dc, 2dc in first chain that has 2dc in it. Join. 26 (28, 32, 36)dc.

Round 2: 1ch, [2dc in dc] twice, 9 (10, 12, 14)dc, [2dc in dc] four times, 9 (10, 12, 14)dc, [2dc in dc] twice. Join. 34 (36, 40, 44)dc.

For size 0–6 months ONLY

Round 3: 1ch, 3dc, 2dc in dc, 9 (-, -, -) dc, [2dc in dc, 1dc] four times, 9 (-, -, -) sts, 2dc in dc, 3dc. Join. 40 (-, -, -)dc.

For sizes 6–12 months, 1 year and 2 years ONLY

Round 3: 1ch, 3htr, 2htr in dc, - (10, 12, 14)htr, [2htr in dc, 1 htr] four times, - (10, 12, 14)htr, 2htr in dc, 3htr. Join. - (42, 46, 50)htr.

For ALL sizes

Round 4: 1ch, 4dc, 2dc in next, 4 (5, 6, 7)dc, 5 (5, 6, 7)htr, 2htr in next, 5htr, 2htr in next, 4htr, 2htr in next, 5 (5, 6, 7)htr, 4 (5, 6, 7)dc, 2dc in next, 4dc. Join. 45 (47, 51, 55) sts.

Round 5: 1ch, 5dc, 2dc in dc, 4 (5, 6, 7) dc, 5 (5, 6, 7)htr, 2htr in htr, 13htr, 2htr in htr, 5 (5, 6, 7)htr, 4 (5, 6, 7)dc, 2dc in next, 5dc. Join. Turn. 49 (51, 55, 59) sts.

Uppers

With outside facing (RS), work 1 (1, 2, 2) rounds even in dc. Join.

Round 2 (2, 3, 3): 1ch, 16 (17, 19, 21) dc, [dc2tog, 1dc] six times, 15 (16, 18, 20) dc. Join. 43 (45, 49, 53)dc.

Work 1 (1, 2, 2) rounds even in dc. Join.

Round 4 (4, 6, 6): 2ch, 15 (16, 18, 20) htr, 2ch, work toe gather (see special stitches), 2ch, miss one, 15 (16, 18, 20)htr. Join. 31 (33, 37, 41) sts.

Round 5 (5, 7, 7): 1ch, working over the elastic, 13 (14, 16, 18)dc, dc2tog, [1dc into ch] twice, 1dc, [1dc into ch] twice, dc2tog, 13 (14, 16, 18)dc. Join. 33 (35, 39, 43)dc.

Fastening

Slipper 1: Turn. 9 (10, 10, 11)slst, 20 (22, 24, 26)ch, 1slst into next. Break yarn and weave in ends.

Slipper 2: 9 (10, 10, 11)slst, 20 (22, 24, 26)ch, 1slst into next. Break yarn and weave in ends.

Sew on button on opposite side to ch loop, approximately two stitches back from the toe gather.

HEDGEHOG MITTENS

These little mittens are perhaps my favourite of all my designs
(just don't tell the others).

skill level: intermediate

Size	Small	Medium	Large
Hand circumference	12cm	15cm	18cm
Hand length	14cm	16cm	18cm
Yarn amounts	72m	109m	153m

MATERIALS:
- Main Colour (MC): 1 (1, 2) x 25g balls of Jamieson's Shetland Spindrift, 4ply (100 per cent Shetland wool), 105m Moorit (108)
- Contrast Colour (CC): 1 x 25g ball of Jamieson's Shetland Spindrift, 4ply (100 per cent Shetland wool), 105m Mogit (107)
- 3mm hook
- 2.5mm hook
- Embroidery needle
- Small amount of black embroidery floss or thin black yarn for eyes and nose
- Stitch marker

YARN REVIEW:
This 4ply yarn comes straight from the islands of Shetland; there are over 160 colours in the range and its lovely tweedy texture is perfect for this project.

YARN ALTERNATIVES:
Rowan Fine Tweed

TENSION:
Work 24 sts and ten rounds in double crochet to measure 10cm square using a 3mm hook, or size required to obtain tension.

SPECIAL STITCHES:
Bobble Stitch (BS)
[YO, insert hook into stitch, YO and pull through, YO and pull through two loops on the hook] four times. YO and pull through remaining five loops on the hook.

Pattern notes: This pattern is worked entirely in the round in the amigurumi style, with no seams or turning chains at the start of the rounds. Use a stitch marker to mark the beginning of each round.

Do not turn your work at the end of each round.

INSTRUCTIONS:

With larger hook and CC, make 1ch, 6dc into a magic loop. (6)dc.

Round 1: *2dc into dc; repeat from * around. (12)dc.

Round 2: 12dc.

Round 3: *1dc, 2dc into dc; repeat from * around. (18)dc.

Round 4: 18dc.

Round 5: *2dc, 2dc into dc; repeat from * around. (24)dc.

Round 6: 24dc.

For Small size, break yarn and continue to the Body section.

For sizes Medium and Large ONLY

Round 7: *3dc, 2dc into dc; repeat from * around. (30)dc.

Round 8: 30dc.

For Medium size, break yarn and continue to the Body section.

For size Large ONLY

Round 9: *4dc, 2dc into dc; repeat from * around. (36)dc.

Round 10: 36dc.

Break yarn, continue to the Body section.

Body
For ALL sizes

Tip: when working the odd number rounds, move the stitch marker one stitch to the left at the end of the round to keep the BS in line with those of the previous rounds.

Join MC.

Round 1: 24 (30, 36)dc.

Round 2: [1dc, 1BS] six (eight, nine) times, 1dc, 11 (13, 17)tr. 24 (30, 36) sts.

Rounds 3–8 (10, 12): repeat rounds 1–2. 24 (30, 36) sts.

For Left Mitten

Round 9 (11, 13): 13 (17, 19)dc, 6 (6, 7)ch, miss 4 (4, 5), 7 (9, 12)dc. 20 (26, 31)dc.

For Right Mitten

Round 9 (11, 13): 19 (25, 30)dc, 6 (6, 7)ch, miss 4 (4, 5), 1dc. 20 (26, 31)dc.

Round 10 (12, 14): [1dc, 1BS] six (eight, nine) times, dc across, working 1dc into each ch from the previous round. 26 (32, 38) sts.

Round 11 (13, 15): 26 (32, 38)dc.

Round 12 (14, 16): 26 (32, 38)tr.

Rounds 13 (15, 17) – 16 (18, 20): Switch to the smaller hook, *RtrF, RtrB; repeat from * to end. Break yarn and weave in ends.

Thumb

Round 1: Re-attach MC yarn at the first missed stitch for the thumbhole. Work dc around the thumb opening, working into the missed stitches and then into the spaces between the tr stitches on the other side of the thumb opening. 10 (10, 12)dc.

Rounds 2–4 (4, 5): 10 (10, 12)dc.

Round 5 (5, 6): [3 (3, 4)dc, dc2tog] twice. 8 (8, 10)dc.

Round 6 (6, 7): [2 (2, 3)dc, dc2tog] twice. 6 (6, 8)dc.

For size Large ONLY

Round 8: [2dc, dc2tog] twice. - (-, 6)dc.

For ALL sizes

Break yarn, leaving a 15cm tail. Use the tail and your tapestry needle to sew the top of the thumb closed.

Thread your sewing needle with black embroidery floss and, using the photo as a guide, embroider eyes and nose with a satin stitch.

Weave in ends.

LEG WARMERS

Whether you want to channel your inner *Flashdance* or simply keep the gap between trousers and socks warm, these legwarmers will do the job.

skill level: intermediate

Size	Newborn	Baby	Toddler	4+ years
Circumference	15cm	18cm	20cm	23cm
Length	18cm	19cm	20cm	23cm
Yarn amounts	193m	225.5m	273m	326m

MATERIALS:
- 1 x 100g ball of Zitron Trekking XXL (75 per cent superwash wool, 25 per cent polyamide), 420m Oatmeal (215)
- 3.25mm/D3 hook
- 3.75mm/F5 hook
- Tapestry needle

YARN REVIEW:
This is a Fingering/4ply-weight wool, which when worked with a slightly larger hook than called for creates a warm and soft fabric.

YARN ALTERNATIVES:
Regia Tweed 4ply

TENSION:
Work 10 sts and ten rows in Crossed Puff Stitch pattern to measure 10cm square using a 3.75mm hook, or size required to obtain tension.

SWATCH PATTERN
Make 33ch.

Row 1: Starting in the 7th ch from hook (counts as 3ch tch and 3 missed stitches)1htr, 2ch, 1 Puff Stitch into the first missed stitch, *miss 2 stitches, 1htr in the next stitch, 2ch, Puff Stitch in the same stitch as the 1htr from the previous stitch; repeat from * to end. Join. Turn. (10)Crossed Puff Stitches.

Rows 2–10: 4ch, miss 2, 1htr, 2ch, 1Puff Stitch into the same stitch as the slst join from the previous round, * miss 2 stitches, 1htr in the next stitch, 2ch, Puff Stitch in the same stitch as the 1htr from the previous stitch; repeat from * to end. Join. Turn. (10)Crossed Puff Stitches.

SPECIAL STITCHES

Puff Stitch (PS)

[YO, insert hook into stitch and draw up a loop] twice (five loops on hook). YO and pull through four loops on hook.

Crossed Puff Stitch (CPS)

First stitch: 2ch, miss 2 stitches, 1htr in the next stitch, 2ch, PS into bottom of the 2ch before the 2 missed stitches. (1) CPS.

Following stitches: 2ch, miss 2 stitches, 1htr in the next stitch, 2ch, PS into the same stitch as the previous htr before the 2 missed stitches. (1)CPS.

INSTRUCTIONS (Make 2):

With the smaller hook, make 46 (52, 60, 66)ch. Join in the round.

Round 1: 3ch, 46 (52, 60, 66)tr. Join. 46 (52, 60, 66)tr.

Rounds 2–3: 3ch, *RtrF, RtrB; repeat from * to end. Join. 46 (52, 60, 66) sts.

Round 4: 4ch, miss 3 (3, 2, 2), 1htr, 2ch, 1PS into the same stitch as the slst join from the previous round, *miss 2 stitches, 1htr in the next stitch, 2ch, PS in the same stitch as the 1htr from the previous stitch; repeat from * to end. Join. Turn. 15 (17, 20, 22)CPS.

Rounds 5–15 (16, 17, 20): 3ch, 15 (17, 20, 22)CPS. Join. Turn. 15 (17, 20, 22)CPS.

Round 16 (17, 18, 21): 3ch, 4tr, *3tr, miss one; repeat from * to end. Join. 46 (52, 60, 66)tr.

Rounds 17 (18, 19, 22) – 18 (19, 20, 23): repeat rounds 2–3.

Break yarn and weave in tails.

Pattern notes: Do not count the 3ch at the beginning of the round as a stitch. Do not turn the rounds when working the cuff ribbing. Turn the rounds when working the CPS pattern.

MERMAID TAIL

New babies spend so very much of their time asleep.
A sweet little mermaid tail not only keeps them warm,
but makes for some adorable new baby photos.

MATERIALS:

- 1 x 250g hank of Cascade Eco+ (100 per cent Peruvian wool), 437m Pacific (2433)
- 5mm/H8 hook
- 5.5mm/I9 hook
- Tapestry needle
- 2 x buttons (2.5cm in diameter)
- Stitch marker

YARN REVIEW:

This is a warm, chunky yarn, which makes this a quick project. The colour has hints of silver, making it sparkle like the sea.

YARN ALTERNATIVES:

Wendy Mode Chunky

TENSION:

Work 14 sts and 13 rows in double crochet ribbing to measure 10cm square using a 5mm hook, or size required to obtain tension.

Work 2.5 sts and seven rows in shell stitch to measure 10cm square using a 5.5mm hook, or size required to obtain tension.

SPECIAL STITCHES:

Shell Stitch (Sh)

Set-up row: Miss 2 stitches, 5tr in same stitch, miss 2 stitches, 1dc in next stitch.
Subsequent rows: 1dc in 3rd tr of shell, 5tr in dc.

Shell Decrease (Sh dec)

5tr into dc from previous round. Insert your hook into the 3rd tr of the shell from the previous round, YO and draw up a loop. Insert your hook into the next dc, YO, draw up a loop, insert the hook into the 3rd tr of the next shell, YO and draw up a loop. YO and pull through all four loops on the hook.

PATTERN NOTES:

This sleep sack is as cute as can be, but is also practical. The waistband is worked first in ribbing, then the scallop stitch is worked directly onto the ribbing, first in rows then joined in the round from the top down. A series of increases and decreases are made for the tail, before stitching it closed and constructing the fins.

skill level:
intermediate

Size	0–6 months
Finished waist	41–46cm
Finished length	66cm
Yarn amounts	299m

INSTRUCTIONS:

Waistband

Using the smaller hook, make 10ch.

Row 1(RS): Starting in the 2nd chain from the hook, 9dc. (9)dc.

Rows 2–3: 1ch, 9dc in BLO. Turn. (9)dc.

Row 4: Turn, 1ch, 1dc, 2ch, miss 2 sts, 3dc in BLO, miss 2 sts, 1dc. (5)dc.

Rows 5–6: 1ch, 9dc in BLO. Turn. (9)dc.

Row 7: Turn, 1ch, 1dc in BLO, 2ch, miss 2 sts, 3dc in BLO, miss 2 sts, 1dc in BLO, (5)dc.

Rows 8–64: 1ch, 9dc in BLO. Turn. (9) dc.

Tail set-up row: Without breaking the yarn, turn your work so you can work across the ribbing, RS facing. 54dc, working one stitch into the end of each row for 54 rows. Turn. (54)dc.

Tail

Row 1: Using the larger hook, 1ch, 1dc, 9Sh, miss 2 stitches, 1dc. Turn. (9)Sh.

Row 2: 3ch (counts as 1tr), 2tr in first dc, 9Sh 3tr in last dc. Turn. (9)Sh.

Row 3: 1ch, 1dc, 9Sh. Turn. (9)Sh.

Row 4: As Row 2. Do not turn.

You will now start working in rounds. Mark the start of the round with a stitch marker.

Round 1: Fold work in half and dc into the top of the first 3ch in the previous row. This will connect the work into the round. *2Sh, [3tr, 1ch, 1dc, 1ch, 3tr] into same stitch; repeat from * around. (9)Sh.

Round 2: *3Sh, place the dc from the 3rd Sh in the 2nd (centre) tr of the 1st tr cluster you created, 5tr into the next dc, dc into the 2nd tr of the next tr cluster; repeat from * around. (12)Sh.

Rounds 3–21: Work even in established shell pattern, making 1dc in the 3rd tr of the shell stitch from the previous round, 5tr into the next dc of the previous round.

Round 22: (1Sh dec, 4Sh) twice. (10)Sh.

Rounds 23–24: Work even in established shell pattern.

Round 25: (3Sh,1Sh dec) twice. (8)Sh.

Rounds 26–27: Work even in established shell pattern.

Round 28: (1Sh dec, 1Sh) twice. (6)Sh.

Rounds 29–30: Work even in established shell pattern.

Round 31: (1Sh, 1Sh dec) twice. (4)Sh.

Round 32: Work even in established shell pattern.

Finishing: Line up the tail so that the

slit at the waistband is just slightly off to one side. Flatten. Dc the tail closed at the bottom. Do not break yarn.

Fin

Work all dc stitches in the fin into BLO. Using the larger hook, 21ch.

Row 1: Starting with the 2nd chain from hook, 20dc back up to the tail. Join into the same stitch that the ch starts from. Turn. (20)dc.

Row 2: Slst into the next dc of the tail (counts as tch), 18dc. Turn. (18)dc.

Row 3: 1ch, 11dc, dc2tog, 5dc back up to tail. Join into the same stitch as slst. Turn. (17)dc.

Row 4: Slst into the next dc of the tail (counts as tch), 5dc, dc2tog, 9dc. Turn. (15)dc.

Row 5: 1ch, 9dc, dc2tog, 3dc back up to tail. Join into the same stitch as slst. Turn. (13)dc.

Row 6: Slst into the next dc of the tail (counts as tch), 3dc, dc2tog, 8dc. Turn. (12)dc.

Row 7: 1ch, 7dc, dc2tog, 3dc back up to tail. Join into the same stitch as slst. Break yarn. (11)dc.

Join wool at opposite side of end of tail. Repeat Fin rows 1–7. Do not break yarn. Slst the two halves of the fin together. Break yarn and weave in tails.

Buttons

The buttons are sewn on approx. 1cm away from the edge on the end of the ribbing that does not have buttonholes. Use the buttonholes for a guide on the placement. The two sets of buttonholes allow you to expand the waist of the sleep sack as the baby grows.

TUTU

There are certain wardrobe items that (sadly) children can pull off that adults can't. Tutus are on that list.

skill level: intermediate

Size	1 year	2 years	4 years	6 years
Finished waist	53cm	54.5cm	56cm	58cm
Finished length	16cm	18cm	25cm	28cm
Yarn amounts	485m	506m	666m	713m

MATERIALS:
- 6 (6, 8, 8) x 50g balls of Sirdar Snuggly Baby Bamboo DK (80 per cent bamboo, 20 per cent wool), 95m Flip Flop (125)
- 54 (55, 57, 58)cm of 2cm wide elastic webbing sewn securely in a loop for waist band.
- 4mm/G6 hook
- Tapestry needle
- Stitch marker

YARN REVIEW:
Baby Bamboo is one of my favourite yarns to use for babies and toddlers, as it's lovely to work with and washes extremely well. Combine this with the shimmer and luxury of bamboo and you have simply a lovely DK-weight yarn.

YARN ALTERNATIVES:
Rowan Baby Silk Merino DK
Fyberspates Scrumptious DK

TENSION:
Work 17 sts and 23 rows in double crochet to measure 10cm square using a 4mm hook, or size required to obtain tension.

Pattern notes: Do not count the 1ch at the beginning of the round or row as a stitch. Do not turn your work at the end of each round.

INSTRUCTIONS:

90 (92, 94, 98)ch. Join in the round.

Waistband

Rounds 1–17: 1ch, 90 (92, 94, 98)dc. Join. 90 (92, 94, 98)dc.

Round 18: Fold the waistband in half, long edges aligned, insert your elastic webbing into the opening. Working through all four loops, dc the waistband closed with the elastic inside.

Skirt

Round 19: (It may help to add a stitch marker here to find the back loops when you come back to work on the Drop underskirt.) Working in the FLO of the previous round, 1ch, ★1dc, 2dc in dc; repeat from ★ around. Join. 135 (138, 141, 147)dc.

Rounds 20–33 (36, 39, 42): 1ch, 1dc in each stitch around. Join. 135 (138, 141, 147)dc.

Drop Underskirt

Round 34 (37, 40, 43): Break yarn and re-attach into the back loops at the beginning of the round where you worked the skirt into the front loops. Working in BLO, 1ch, 90 (92, 94, 98)dc. Join. 90 (92, 94, 98)dc.

Rounds 35 (38, 41, 44) – 39 (43, 47, 51): 1ch, 90 (92, 94, 98)dc. Join. 90 (92, 94, 98)dc.

Repeat rounds 19–39 (43, 47, 51) two (two, three, three) times.

Repeat rounds 19–33 (36, 39, 42) once. Weave in ends.

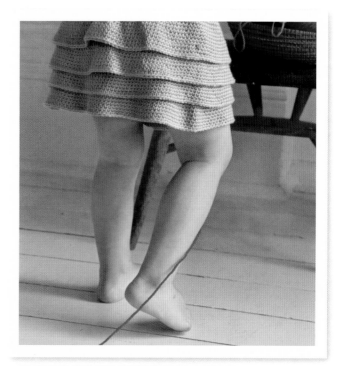

WHOLE
SELF

Cabled Yoke Cardigan
The Professor
Rainbow Bright
Silver Birch Tunic
Wolf

CABLED YOKE CARDIGAN

The swirling horizontal cable on this cardigan adds a touch of elegance and interest to a basic staple of a baby's wardrobe.

skill level: intermediate

Size	Newborn	0-6 months	6-12 months	1 year
Chest circumference	48.5cm	50cm	56cm	60cm
Yarn amounts	199m	217m	279m	319m

MATERIALS:
- 2 (3, 3, 4) x 50g balls of Sirdar Snuggly Baby Bamboo DK (80 per cent bamboo, 20 per cent wool), 95m Warm Grey (170))
- 6 (7, 7, 8) x buttons (approx. 0.5cm in diameter)
- 4mm/G6 hook
- Tapestry needle
- Sewing needle
- Thread

YARN REVIEW:
A blend of bamboo and wool, this lovely silky DK-weight yarn is both elegant and washable – perfect for children's wear.

YARN ALTERNATIVES:
King Cole Bamboo Cotton DK
Sublime Baby Silk and Bamboo Yarn DK

TENSION:
Work 17 sts and 23 rows in double crochet to measure 10cm square using a 4mm hook, or size required to obtain tension.

Pattern note: The cable is worked first, with the decreases from the cable to the neck built on top and the chest and sleeves picked up around the bottom.

INSTRUCTIONS:

Cable

Make 10ch.

Row 1 (RS): Starting in the 4th ch from hook, 7tr. Turn. (8) sts.

Row 2: 3ch (counts as a stitch), 6RtrB, 1tr. Turn. (8) sts.

Row 3: 3ch, miss 3, 3RdtrF, 3RdtrF in the 3 missed stitches, 1tr in the last stitch. Turn. (8) sts.

Row 4: repeat row 2.

Row 5: 3ch, 6RtrF, 1tr. Turn. (8) sts. Work rows 2–5 18 (20, 21, 22) times.

Cable to Neck Decreases

Do not count the chain stitches at the beginning of the row as a stitch, unless indicated.

Turn your work, so you can work along the long edge, WS facing.

Row 1 (WS): 1ch, 1dc into the end of each row. Turn. 72 (80, 84, 88)dc.

Row 2: 1ch, 0 (2, 0, 4)dc, [10 (11, 12, 12)dc, dc2tog] six times. Turn. 66 (74, 78, 82)dc.

Row 3: 1ch, 0 (2, 0, 4)dc, [9 (10, 11, 11)dc, dc2tog] six times. Turn. 60 (68, 72, 76)dc.

Row 4: 1ch, 0 (2, 0, 4)dc, [8 (9, 10, 10)dc, dc2tog] six times. Turn. 54 (62, 66, 70)dc.

Row 5: 1ch, 0 (2, 0, 4)dc, [7 (8, 9, 9)dc, dc2tog] six times. Turn. 48 (56, 60, 64)dc.

Row 6: 1ch, 0 (2, 0, 4)dc, [6 (7, 8, 8)dc, dc2tog] six times. Turn. 42, (50, 54, 58)dc.

Row 7: 1ch, 0 (2, 0, 4)dc, [5 (6, 9, 9)dc, dc2tog] six times. Turn. 36 (44, 48, 52)dc.

For Newborn size, go to row 9.

For sizes 0–6 months, 6–12 months and 1 year ONLY

Row 8: 1ch, - (2, 0, 4)dc, [- (5, 8, 8)dc, dc2tog] six times. Turn. - (38, 42, 46)dc.

For ALL sizes

Row 9: 2ch (counts as 1 stitch), [miss 1, tr in the next, tr in the missed stitch] repeat across 17 (18, 20, 22) times, tr in the last stitch. Turn. 36 (38, 42, 46)tr. Break yarn. Turn your work and rejoin your yarn at the long edge of the bottom of the cable, WS facing.

Chest

Row 1(WS): 1ch (does not count as a stitch), working into the ends of each row [1dc, 2dc into the next] 36 (40, 42, 44) times. Turn. 108 (120, 126, 132)dc.

Row 2: 1ch, work dc across, increase 10 (0, 6, 8) stitches evenly spaced across the row. Turn. 118 (120, 132, 140)dc.

Split the Body and Sleeves

Row 3: 1ch, 17 (17, 20, 21)dc, 6 (7, 8, 8) fdc, miss 24 (25, 26, 28), 36 (36, 40, 42)dc, 6 (7, 8, 8)fdc, miss 24 (25, 26, 28), 17 (17, 20, 21)dc. Turn. 82 (84, 96, 100) sts.

Rows 4–26 (28, 32, 34): 1ch, 82 (84, 96, 100)dc. Turn.

Edging

Row 1: 2ch, ★miss 1, tr in the next, tr in the missed stitch; repeat across 40 (41, 47, 49) times, tr in the last stitch. 82 (84, 96, 100)tr.

Row 2: 1ch, 82 (84, 96, 100)dc. Turn.

Row 3: 2ch, 82 (84, 96, 100)tr. Turn.

Row 4: 2ch, ★RtrF, RtrB; repeat from ★ around.

Break yarn and weave in ends.

Sleeves (Make 2)

With RS facing, rejoin yarn in the middle of the fdc made for the armholes.

Round 1(RS): 24 (26, 34, 36): 1ch, 30 (31, 34, 36)dc. Join. Turn. 30 (31, 34, 36)dc.

Sleeve Edging

Round 1: 2ch (counts as 1 stitch), ★miss 1, tr in the next, tr in the missed stitch; repeat across 14 (15, 16, 17) times. For 0–6 months, 6–12 months and 1 year only: tr in the last stitch. Turn. 30 (31, 34, 36)dc.

Round 2: 1ch, 30 (31, 34, 36)dc. Join. Turn.

Round 3: 2ch, 29 (30, 33, 35)tr. Join. Turn.

Round 4: 2 ch (counts as a stitch)★RtrF, RtrB; repeat from ★ around.

Break yarn and weave in ends.

Buttonholes

For boys' garments, buttonholes are worked on the right side of the garment and girls' buttonholes are worked on the left.

Row 1: Join yarn at the front edge of the garment, RS facing on the side where you want to work the buttonholes. Make 1dc into the end of each dc row, 2dc into the end of each tr row and 1 stitch into each stitch in the cable section up to the neck. Turn. 48 (51, 55, 57)dc.

Row 2 (WS): 1ch, 3 (1, 3, 1)dc, ★1ch, miss 1, 5dc; repeat from around 6 (7, 7, 8) times, 2 (1, 3, 1)dc. 42 (44, 48, 49)dc. Break yarn and weave in ends.

Buttonband

Row 1: Join yarn at the front edge of the garment, on the opposite side to where you are working your buttonholes. Make 1dc into the end of each dc row, 2dc into the end of each tr row and 1 stitch into each stitch in the cable section up to the neck. Turn. 48 (51, 55, 57)dc.

Row 2: 1ch, 41 (44, 48, 50)dc. Break yarn and weave in ends. Using the buttonholes as a guide, sew buttons securely into place using sewing needle and thread.

THE PROFESSOR

Vests with cables and shawl collars are one of my favourite garments to make and wear. I love the way they accentuate the little old man factor in babies, whilst also being practical, keeping their core bodies and little necks warm.

skill level: intermediate

Size	0–6 months	6–12 months	1 year	2 years	4 years	6 years
Finished chest	47cm	52cm	54cm	57cm	64cm	69cm
Finished length	24cm	26cm	28cm	30cm	32cm	36cm
Yarn amounts	281m	339m	404m	451m	497m	611m

MATERIALS:
- 3 (3, 4, 4, 5, 6) x 50g balls of Sublime Extra Fine Merino Wool DK (100 per cent merino wool), 116m Mocha (020)
- 4mm/G6 hook
- 4 x buttons (2.5cm in diameter)
- Tapestry needle

YARN REVIEW:
Sumptuous, with great stitch definition, this DK-weight superwash merino is the perfect mix of luxury and wearability.

YARN ALTERNATIVES:
Wendy Merino DK
MillaMia Naturally Soft Merino

TENSION:
Work 20 sts and 14 rows in basket weave (see special stitches) to measure 10cm square using a 4mm/G6 hook, or size required to obtain tension.
Work 20 sts and 20 rows in double crochet ribbing (see special stitches) to measure 10cm square using 4mm/G6 hook, or size required to obtain tension.

SPECIAL STITCHES:

Basket Weave

Basket weave stitch is created by alternating sets of RtrF and RtrB stitches in groups of four to create stitches that pop out or recede on alternate sides of the fabric. After four rows of raising the stitches on one side, alternate the direction of the raised stitches to push the stitches out on the other side of the garment.

For multiples of eight stitches:

Row 1: *4RtrF, 4RtrB; repeat from * across. Turn.

Row 2: *4RtrB, 4RtrF; repeat from * across. Turn.

Row 3: repeat row 1.

Row 4: repeat row 2.

Row 5: repeat row 2.

Row 6: repeat row 1.

Row 7: repeat row 2.

Row 8: repeat row 1.

Repeat rows 1–8.

Double Crochet Ribbing

Rows of dc are worked into the BLO.

PATTERN NOTES:

- You will maintain the stitch pattern throughout.
- Do not count the chains at the beginning of the row as a stitch.

INSTRUCTIONS:

Make 50 (54, 58, 62, 66, 74)ch.

Row 1 (WS): Starting in the 3rd ch from hook, 48 (52, 56, 60, 64, 72)tr. Turn. 48 (52, 56, 60, 64, 72) sts.

Rows 2–5 (5, 7, 7, 7, 9): 2ch, work in basket weave pattern. Turn. 48 (52, 56, 60, 64, 72) sts.

Rows 6 (6, 8, 8, 8, 10) – 13 (13, 15, 15, 17, 19): 2ch, 28 (32, 36, 36, 40, 44) stitches in basket weave pattern. Turn. 28 (32, 36, 36, 40, 44) sts.

Row 14 (14, 16, 16, 18, 20): 2ch, 28 (32, 36, 36, 40, 44) stitches in basket weave pattern. 22 (22, 22, 26, 26, 30)ch. Turn. 28 (32, 36, 36, 40, 44) sts.

Row 15 (15, 17, 17, 19, 21): Starting in 3rd ch from hook, work 20 (20, 20, 24, 24, 28)tr into the chain, continue in basket weave pattern. Turn. 48 (52, 56, 60, 64, 72) sts.

Rows 16 (16, 18, 18, 20, 22) – 19 (19, 23, 23, 25, 29): 2ch, work in basket weave pattern. Turn. 48 (52, 56, 60, 64, 72) sts.

Row 20 (20, 24, 24, 26, 30): 4slst, 2ch, work in basket weave pattern. Turn. 44 (48, 52, 56, 60, 68) sts.

Rows 21 (21, 25, 25, 27, 31) – 31 (35, 37, 39, 43, 47): 2ch, work in basket weave pattern. Turn. 44 (48, 52, 56, 60, 68) sts.

Row 32 (36, 38, 40, 44, 48): 2ch, work in basket weave pattern. 6ch. 44 (48, 52, 56, 60, 68) sts.

Row 33 (37, 39, 41, 45, 49): Starting in 3rd ch from hook, work 4htr into the chain, continue in basket weave pattern. Turn. 48 (52, 56, 60, 64, 72) sts.

Rows 34 (38, 40, 42, 46, 50) – 37 (41, 45, 47, 51, 57): 2ch, work in basket weave pattern. Turn. 48 (52, 56, 60, 64, 72) sts.

Rows 38 (42, 46, 48, 52, 58) – 45 (49, 53, 55, 61, 67): 2ch, 28 (32, 36, 36, 40, 44) stitches in basket weave pattern. Turn. 28 (32, 36, 36, 40, 44) sts.

Row 46 (50, 54, 56, 62, 68): 2ch, 28 (32, 36, 36, 40, 44) stitches in basket weave pattern. 22 (22, 22, 26, 26, 30)ch. Turn. 28 (32, 36, 36, 40, 44) sts.

Row 47 (51, 55, 57, 63, 69): Starting in 3rd ch from hook, work 20 (20, 20, 24, 24, 28)tr into the chain, continue in basket weave pattern. Turn. 48 (52, 56, 60, 64, 72) sts.

Rows 48 (52, 56, 58, 64, 70) – 51 (55, 61, 63, 69, 77): 2ch, work in basket weave pattern. Turn. 48 (52, 56, 60, 64, 72) sts.

Break yarn and weave in ends.

Sewing Up

Lay the finished piece flat, with RS up (the original chained edge to the right, shoulders up). Fold the outer edges in, so that the shoulder 'straps' line up. Dc the seams closed, weave in ends. Turn garment right side out.

Shawl Edge Ribbing

Rejoin yarn at the bottom front corner of garment (on the edge with the original chain, if you are making for a girl and on the final row if you are making for a boy). Work 1dc into the end of each row up the sides of the vest and around the neckline to create an even base for the

ribbing. 121 (131, 139, 149, 157, 173)dc.
Make 17 (19, 21, 25, 23, 27)ch.

Row 1: Starting with the 2nd chain
from the hook, 16 (18, 20, 24, 22, 26)dc,
1slst in the first dc of the dc edging on
the lapel. Turn. 16 (18, 20, 24, 22, 26)dc.

Row 2: 1slst into the next dc on the lapel
(counts as tch). 16 (18, 20, 24, 22, 26)dc
BLO. Turn. 16 (18, 20, 24, 22, 26)dc.

Row 3: 1ch, 16 (18, 20, 24, 22, 26)dc
BLO. Slst in the first dc of the dc edging
on the lapel. Turn. 16 (18, 20, 24, 22, 26)
dc.

**Rows 4–121 (131, 139, 149,
157, 173):** Repeat rows 2–3. Work
buttonhole on rows 6 (8, 8, 8, 10, 10)
and 18 (20, 20, 20, 22, 22) as follows:
Slst into next dc on the lapel (counts as
tch). 3 (4, 4, 6, 5, 6)dc BLO, 3ch, miss 3,
(4, 6, 6, 6, 8)dc BLO, 3ch, miss 3, (4, 4, 6,
5, 6) BLO. Turn. 10 (12, 14, 18, 16, 20).

RAINBOW BRIGHT

This quick and fun little dress makes a bold statement with its geometric shapes and bright colours. It is sized in a way that means that it can start as a dress and become a top as the child grows.

skill level: intermediate

Size	0-6 months	6-12 months	1 year	2 years	4 years	6 years
Finished chest	52cm	56cm	59cm	61cm	68cm	74cm
Finished length	32cm	33cm	34cm	36cm	38cm	41cm
Yarn amounts	231m	263m	298m	323m	385m	427m

MATERIALS:
- Main Colour (MC): 3 (4, 4, 4, 5, 6) x 50g balls of Rico Creative Cotton Aran (100 per cent cotton), 85m Mouse (28)
- Colour A: 1 x 50g ball of Rico Creative Cotton Aran (100 per cent cotton), 85m Red (05)
- Colour B: 1 x 50g ball of Rico Creative Cotton Aran (100 per cent cotton), 85m Orange (74)
- Colour C: 1 x 50g ball of Rico Creative Cotton Aran (100 per cent cotton), 85m Banana (63)
- Colour D: 1 x 50g ball of Rico Creative Cotton Aran (100 per cent cotton), 85m Green (49)
- Colour E: 1 x 50g ball of Rico Creative Cotton Aran (100 per cent cotton), 85m Royal (39)
- 5mm/H8 hook
- 4.5mm/7 hook
- Stitch marker
- Tapestry needle

YARN REVIEW:
The colours in this range of affordable cotton yarn are so vibrant, it is hard to pick just one...

YARN ALTERNATIVES:
Knit Picks Simply Cotton Worsted Yarn

TENSION:
Work 8.25 sts and 16 rows in tweed stitch to measure 10cm square using a 5mm hook, or size required to obtain tension.

SPECIAL STITCHES:
Tweed Stitch
Set-up round: 1ch, *1dc, 1ch, miss 1; repeat from * across.
All other rounds: 1ch, *1dc into chsp, 1ch; repeat from * across.

PATTERN NOTES:
• Do not count the chains at the beginning of the round as a stitch.
• Do not turn your work at the end of each round.

INSTRUCTIONS:
Yoke
Using the larger hook, make 56 (60, 64, 68, 72, 76)ch. Join in the round with a slst.
Row 1: 2ch, 56 (60, 64, 68, 72, 76)htr. Join.
Row 2: 2ch, [3htr, 2htr in htr] 14 (15, 16, 17, 18, 19) times. Join. 70 (75, 80, 85, 90, 95)htr.
Row 3: 2ch, 70 (75, 80, 85, 90, 95)htr. Join.

Row 4: 2ch, [4htr, 2htr into htr] 14 (15, 16, 17, 18, 19) times. Join. 84 (90, 96, 102, 108, 114)htr.

For sizes 0–6 months and 6–12 months go to round 1 of the Bodice.

For sizes 1 year, 2 years, 4 years and 6 years ONLY
Row 5: 2ch, - (-, 96, 102, 108, 114)htr. Join.

For sizes 1 year and 2 years, continue to Round 1 of the Bodice.

For sizes 4 years and 6 years ONLY
Row 6: 2ch, [5htr, 2htr into htr] - (-, -, -, 18, 18) times. - (-, -, -, 0, 6)htr. Join. - (-, -, -, 126, 132)htr.

Bodice
Round 1 (this round is worked in BLO): Continuing in MC, 1ch, [1dc, 1ch, miss 1] 14 (15, 16, 17, 21, 22) times, make 12 (14, 14, 14, 12, 14)fdc, miss 14 (15, 16, 17, 21, 22), [1dc, 1ch, miss 1] 14 (15, 16, 17, 21, 22) times, make 12 (14, 14, 14, 12, 14)fdc, miss 14 (15, 16, 17, 21, 22). Join in the round. Break yarn. 52 (58, 60, 62, 66, 72)dc.
Round 2: Join Colour A and mark beginning of round with a stitch marker, 1ch, [1dc, 1ch, miss 1] 6 (7, 7, 7, 6, 7) times, [1dc into chsp, 1ch] 14 (15, 16, 17, 21, 22) times, [1dc, 1ch, miss 1] 6 (7, 7, 7, 6, 7) times, [1dc into chsp, 1ch] 14 (15, 16, 17, 21, 22) times. Join. Break yarn. 40 (44, 46, 48, 54, 58)dc.
Round 3: Switch to MC, 1ch, [1dc, 1ch,

1dc] into the same chsp, 1ch, [1dc into chsp, 1ch] 20 (22, 23, 24, 27, 29) times, [1dc, 1ch, 1dc] into the same chsp, 1ch, [1dc into chsp, 1ch] 20 (22, 23, 24, 27, 29) times. Join. Break yarn. 42 (46, 48, 50, 56, 60).
Round 4: Switch to Colour B: 1ch, work in tweed stitch around. Join. Break yarn. 42 (46, 48, 50, 56, 60).
Rounds 5–43 (45, 47, 49, 51, 53): repeat round 4, changing the colours in pattern. The colour pattern in this section is worked as follows:
Round 5: MC
Round 6: Colour C
Round 7: MC
Round 8: Colour D
Round 9: MC
Round 10: Colour E
Round 11: MC
Round 12: Colour A
Round 13: MC
Round 14: Colour B
Repeat as required.
Rounds 44 (46, 48, 50, 52, 54) – 47 (49, 52, 54, 57, 59): switch to the smaller hook, 2ch, working 1htr into each ch sp and each dc, 84 (92, 96, 100, 112, 120) htr. Join.
Break yarn and weave in ends.

SILVER BIRCH TUNIC

Inspired by the forests of Scotland in spring, this yoke-necked tunic dress can be made in a variety of ways to suit the seasons. The stitch pattern on the sleeves and dress reminds me of the dappled light coming through the branches of a tree.

skill level: intermediate

Size	3 months	6 months	1 year	2 years	4 years	6 years
Finished chest	48cm	51cm	53cm	56cm	62cm	68.5cm
Finished length	30.5cm	33cm	34cm	37cm	39cm	42cm
Yarn amounts: Yoke	90m	105m	125m	140m	170m	195m
Yarn amounts: Bodice	275m	340m	365m	415m	510m	620m

MATERIALS:

For a Solid Colour Dress

- 2 (2, 2, 3, 3, 4) x 100g hanks Yarn Love Amy March (100 per cent superwash merino), 247m Earl Grey

For a Multi-coloured Dress

- Yoke: 1 x 100g hank Yarn Love Amy March (100 per cent superwash merino), 247m Bouquet
- Bodice and Sleeves: 3 (3, 3, 4, 5, 5) x 50g ball Rowan Pure Wool DK (100 per cent superwash wool), 125m Earth (018)
- 2 x buttons (2.5cm in diameter)
- Tapestry needle
- 4mm/G6 hook

YARN REVIEW:

A beautiful hand-dyed yarn, this DK-weight superwash merino is a beautiful option for a full dress, or adds a bit of luxury at the yoke to a dress made out of a more commercially available wool.

YARN ALTERNATIVES:

King Cole Merino Blend DK
Patons Merino DK

TENSION:

Work 17.5 sts and 20.5 rows in double crochet ribbing (through the back loop) to measure 10cm square using a 4mm hook, or size required to obtain tension.

Work 7.5 sts and 15.5 rows in Angled Crochet to measure 10cm square using a 4mm hook, or size required to obtain tension.

SPECIAL STITCHES:

Angled Crochet (AC)
Work (dc, 2ch, dc) into the 2ch space from the previous row.

Angled Crochet Increase
(dc, 2ch, dc, dc, 2ch, dc) into the 2ch space from the previous row. 1 angled crochet stitch increased.

Pattern notes: This pattern is worked from the top down from the yoke. Sleeves are crocheted on after the bodice is done. There are no seams. To ensure a nicely rounded yoke scatter the increase stitches rather than line them up.

INSTRUCTIONS:

Yoke

In this section, do not count the 1ch at the beginning of the row as a stitch. Using the wool for the yoke, make 44 (48, 49, 51, 55, 59)ch. Turn.

Row 1(RS): Starting in the 2nd ch from hook, 43 (47, 48, 50, 54, 58)dc. Turn. 43 (47, 48, 50, 54, 58)dc.

Rows 2–4: 1ch, work in BLO, dc across, increase by 5 (5, 4, 4, 4, 4) sts evenly across the row. (Increase by working 2dc into dc.) Turn. 58 (62, 60, 62, 66, 70)dc.

Row 5: 1ch, work in BLO, 1dc, 2ch, miss 2, dc across, increase by 5 (5, 4, 4, 4, 4) sts evenly across the row. Turn. 61 (65, 62, 64, 68, 72)dc.

Row 6: 1ch, work in BLO, dc across to missed stitches, increase by 5 (5, 4, 4, 4, 4) sts evenly across the row, 2dc in chsp, 1dc. Turn. 68 (72, 68, 70, 74, 78)dc.

Rows 7–12: As row 2. 98 (102, 92, 94, 98, 102)dc.

For sizes 3 months and 6 months ONLY

Row 13: As row 5. 101 (105, -, -, -, -)dc.
Row 14: As row 6. 108, (112, -, -, -, -)dc.
Rows 15–16: As row 2. 118 (122, -, -, -, -)dc.

For size 3 months ONLY

Break yarn and weave in ends.

For size 6 months ONLY

Rows 17–18: As row 2. - (132, - , -, -, -)dc.
Break yarn and weave in ends.

For sizes 1 year and 2 years ONLY

Rows 13–16: As row 2. - (-, 108, 110, -, -)dc.
Row 17: As row 5. - (-, 110, 112, -, -)dc.
Row 18: As row 6. - (-, 116, 118, -, -)dc.
Rows 19–23: As row 2. - (-, 136, 138, -, -)dc.

For size 1 year ONLY
Break yarn and weave in ends.

For size 2 years ONLY
Row 24: As row 2. - (-, -, 142, -, -)dc.
Break yarn and weave in ends.

For size 4 years and 6 years ONLY
Rows 13–20: As row 2. - (-, -, -, 130, 134)dc.
Row 21: As row 5 - (-, -, -, 132, 136)dc.
Row 22: As row 6. - (-, -, -, 138, 142)dc.
Rows 23–26: As row 2. - (-, -, -, 154, 158)dc.

For size 4 years ONLY
Break yarn and weave in ends.

For size 6 years ONLY
Rows 27–28: As row 2. - (-, -, -, -, 166)dc.
Break yarn and weave in ends.

Bodice
Do not turn your work at the end of each round.
Join yarn for bodice and sleeves on the long edge at the bottom of the yoke, with RS side facing 13 (15, 15, 17, 17, 19) stitches in from the edge with the buttonholes.

Set-up for 3 months
Round 1: (working in BLO) 1ch (does not count as a stitch), [1dc, 2ch, 1dc, miss 1, 1dc, 2ch, 1dc] seven times. 8fdc, miss 22, [1dc, 2ch, 1dc, miss 1, 1dc, 2ch, 1dc] seven times. 8fdc. Missing the remaining 13 stitches from the yoke, join with a slst into the 2ch space at the beginning of

round. (72) sts.
Round 2: 3ch (counts as 1dc and 2ch), dc into same chsp, 13AC, [1dc, 2ch, 1dc] four times across the fdc of the previous round, 14AC, [1dc, 2ch, 1dc] four times across the fdc of the previous round. Join with a slst into the 2ch space at the beginning of round. (36)AC.

Set-up for 6 months
Round 1: (working in BLO) 3ch (counts as 1dc and 2ch), 1dc, [1dc, 2ch, 1dc, miss 1, 1dc, 2ch, 1dc] seven times, 1dc, 2ch, 1dc. 6fdc, miss 25, 1dc, 2ch, 1dc, [1dc, 2ch, 1dc, miss 1, 1dc, 2ch, 1dc] seven times, 1dc, 2ch, 1dc. 6fdc. Missing the remaining 15 stitches from the yoke, join with a slst into the 2ch space at the beginning of round. (76) sts.
Round 2: 3ch (counts as 1dc and 2ch), 1dc into same chsp, 15AC, [1dc, 2ch, 1dc] three times across the fdc of the previous round, 16AC, [1dc, 2ch, 1dc] three times across the fdc of the previous round. Join with a slst into the 2ch space at the beginning of round. (38)AC.

Set-up for 1 year
Round 1: (working in BLO) 1ch (does not count as a stitch), [1dc, 2ch, 1dc, miss 1, 1dc, 2ch, 1dc] eight times. 8fdc, miss 26, [1dc, 2ch, 1dc, miss 1, 1dc, 2ch, 1dc] eight times. 8fdc. Missing the remaining 15 of the stitches from the yoke, join with a slst into the 2ch space at the beginning of round. (80) sts.
Round 2: 3ch (counts as 1dc and 2ch), 1dc into same chsp, 15AC, [1dc, 2ch, 1dc] four times across the fdc of the previous round, 16AC, [1dc, 2ch, 1dc] four times across the fdc of the previous

round. Join with a slst into the 2ch space at the beginning of round. (40)AC.

Set-up for 2 years
Round 1: (working in BLO) 3ch (counts as 1dc and 2ch), 1dc, [1dc, 2ch, 1dc, miss 1, 1dc, 2ch, 1dc] eight times. 8fdc, miss 27, 1dc, 2ch, 1dc, [1dc, 2ch, 1dc, miss 1, 1dc, 2ch, 1dc] eight times. 8fdc. Missing the remaining 15 stitches from the yoke, join with a slst into the 2ch space at the beginning of round. (84) sts.
Round 2: 3ch (counts as 1dc and 2ch), 1dc into same chsp, 16AC, [1dc, 2ch, 1dc] four times across the fdc of the previous round, 17AC, [1dc, 2ch, 1dc] four times across the fdc of the previous round. Join with a slst into the 2ch space at the beginning of round. (42)AC.

Set-up for 4 years
Round 1: (working in BLO) 1ch (does not count as a stitch), [1dc, 2ch, 1dc, miss 1, 1dc, 2ch, 1dc] nine times. 10fdc, miss 30, [1dc, 2ch, 1dc, miss 1, 1dc, 2ch, 1dc] nine times. 10fdc. Missing the remaining 17 stitches from the yoke, join with a slst into the 2ch space at the beginning of round. (92) sts.
Round 2: 3ch (counts as 1dc and 2ch), 1dc into same chsp, 17AC, [1dc, 2ch, 1dc] five times across the fdc of the previous round, 18AC, [1dc, 2ch, 1dc] five times across the fdc of the previous round. Join with a slst into the 2ch space at the beginning of round. (46)AC.

Set-up for 6 years
Round 1: (working in BLO) 3ch (counts as 1dc and 2ch), 1dc [1dc, 2ch, 1dc, miss 1, 1dc, 2ch, 1dc] nine times, 1dc, 2ch, 1dc. 10fdc, miss 32, 1dc, 2ch,

1dc [1dc, 2ch, 1dc, miss 1, 1dc, 2ch, 1dc] nine times, 1dc, 2ch, 1dc. 10fdc. Missing the remaining 18 stitches from the yoke, join with a slst into the 2ch space at the beginning of round. (100) sts.

Round 2: 3ch (counts as 1dc and 2ch), dc into same chsp, 19AC, [1dc, 2ch, 1dc] five times across the fdc of the previous round, 20AC, [1dc, 2ch, 1dc] five times. Join with a slst into the 2ch space at the beginning of round. (50)AC.

For ALL sizes

Rounds 3–7: (3ch (counts as 1dc and 2ch), 1dc) into same chsp. Continue working AC into each 2ch space. Join with a slst into first 2ch space of round. 36 (38, 40, 42, 46, 50)AC.

Round 8: Complete 3 angled crochet increases spaced evenly across the round. 39 (41, 43, 45, 49, 53)AC.

Rounds 9–15: Continue working even in established pattern. 39 (41, 43, 45, 49, 53).

Round 16: Complete 3 angled crochet increases spaced evenly across the round. 42 (44, 46, 48, 52, 56)AC.

Rounds 17–23: Continue working even in established pattern. 42 (44, 46, 48, 52, 56).

Round 24: Complete 3 angled crochet increases spaced evenly across the round. 45 (47, 49, 51, 55, 59)AC.

Rounds 25–31: Continue working even in established pattern. 45 (47, 49, 51, 55, 59).

Round 32: Complete 3 angled crochet increases spaced evenly across the round. 48 (50, 52, 54, 58, 62)AC.

For sizes 3 months, 6 months and 1 year ONLY

Rounds 33–34 (37, 37): Continue working even in established pattern. Break yarn and weave in ends 48 (50, 52, -, -, -)AC.

For sizes 2 years, 4 years and 6 years ONLY

Rounds 33–39: Continue working even in established pattern. - (-, -, 54, 58, 62) AC.

Round 40: Complete 3 angled crochet increases spaced evenly across the round. - (-, -, 57, 61, 65)AC.

For size 2 years ONLY

Round 41: Continue working even in established pattern. Break yarn and weave in ends. - (-, -, 57, -, -)AC.

For sizes 4 years and 6 years ONLY

Rounds 41–42 (45): Work even for specified number of rows. Break yarn and weave in ends. - (-, -, -, 61, 65)AC.

Sleeves

Do not turn your work at the end of each round.

When you work around the yoke section of the sleeves, you will work in the BLO. For the sleeve with the buttonholes, you will overlap 4 (5, 4, 5, 4, 5) stitches from each side, with the buttonholes on top. Pin them into place and work the top layer through the BLO. The underside should be worked through both loops to maintain the line of the stitches and also strengthen the seam.

Set-up for 3 months

Round 1: Join the wool on the middle of the underarm created by the foundation dc. 3ch (counts as 1dc and 2ch), 1dc, miss 1, 1dc, 2ch, 1dc, [1dc, 2ch, 1dc, miss 1, 1dc, 2ch, 1dc] five times. Join with a slst into the 2ch space at the beginning of round. (12)AC.

Set-up for 6 months

Round 1: Join the wool on the middle of the underarm created by the foundation dc. 3ch (counts as 1dc and 2ch), 1dc, miss 1, [1dc, 2ch, 1dc] six times, miss 1, [1dc, 2ch, 1dc] six times, miss 1, 1dc, 2ch, 1dc. Join with a slst into the 2ch space at the beginning of round. (14)AC.

Set-up for 1 year

Round 1: Join the wool on the middle of the underarm created by the foundation dc. 3ch (counts as 1dc and 2ch), 2dc, 2ch, 1dc, [1dc, 2ch, 1dc, miss 1, 1dc, 2ch, 1dc] six times. Join with a slst into the 2ch space at the beginning of round. (14)AC.

Set-up for 2 years

Round 1: Join wool on the middle of the underarm created by the foundation dc. 3ch (counts as 1dc and 2ch), 2dc, 2ch, 1dc, [1dc, 2ch, 1dc, miss 1, 1dc, 2ch, 1dc] five times. 1dc, 2ch, 2dc, 2ch, 2dc, 2ch, 1dc. Join with a slst into the 2ch space at the beginning of round. (15)AC.

Set-up for 4 years

Round 1: Join wool on the middle of the underarm created by the foundation dc. 3ch (counts as 1dc and 2ch), 2dc, 2ch, 1dc, [1dc, 2ch, 1dc, miss 1, 1dc, 2ch, 1dc] seven times, miss 1. Join with a slst into the 2ch space at the beginning of round. (16)AC.

Set-up for 6 years

Round 1: Join wool on the middle of the underarm created by the foundation dc. 3ch (counts as 1dc and 2ch), 1dc [1dc, 2ch, 1dc] two times, [1dc, 2ch, 1dc, miss 1, 1dc, 2ch, 1dc] three times, [1dc, 2ch, 1dc] three times, [1dc, 2ch, 1dc, miss 1, 1dc, 2ch, 1dc] three times. Join with a slst into the 2ch space at the beginning of round. (18) AC.

For ALL sizes

Rounds 2–23 (27, 29, 33, 41, 48): 3ch (counts as dc and 2ch), dc into the same 2ch space. Work AC into each 2ch space. 12 (14, 14, 15, 16, 18).

Fasten off. Using the buttonholes as a guide, sew your buttons onto the appropriate side of the collar. Weave in yarn ends.

WOLF

Cable and ears take a normal hooded jumper and turn it into something rustic. The stodgy half treble stitches are worked in a way that creates a very solid and very warm fabric to keep little beasts snuggly on cold days. It is very generously sized to work over layers and last through growth spurts.

skill level: intermediate

Size	3 months	6 months	1 year	2 years	4 years	6 years
Finished chest	54cm	56cm	67cm	70cm	75cm	78cm
Finished length	34cm	38cm	39cm	41cm	44.5cm	48cm
Sleeve length	16cm	18cm	19cm	22cm	27cm	32cm
Yarn amounts	399m	518m	622m	713m	866m	931m

MATERIALS:
- 4 (5, 6, 7, 8, 9) x 50g balls Artesano Superwash Merino (100 per cent superwash merino), 112m Grey (SFN41)
- 4mm/G6 hook
- Tapestry needle
- 6 (6, 7, 7, 8, 8) toggle-style buttons (approx. 3cm long)

YARN REVIEW:
A fantastically soft DK-weight superwash merino, this lovely yarn works up quickly with a 4mm hook.

YARN ALTERNATIVES:
King Cole Merino Blend DK
Madelinetosh Tosh DK

TENSION:
Work 13 sts and 13 rows in solid half treble (see special stitches) to measure 10cm square using a 4mm hook, or size required to obtain tension.

SPECIAL STITCHES:

Solid Half Treble (shtr)

All of the htr stitches in the pattern are worked into the space between the stitches of the previous row. This creates a more solid, warm fabric and lessens the characteristic striping of crocheting in rows.

Solid Half Treble 2 Together (shtr2tog)

[YO, insert hook into the next space between the stitches, YO and pull through stitch] twice (five loops on hook), YO and pull through all the loops on the hook. One shtr decreased.

Foundation Half Treble Crochet (fhtr)

3ch, YO, insert hook into 3rd ch from hook, YO and pull through (three loops on hook), YO and pull through one loop (1ch made), YO, and draw through all three loops on hook ★YO, insert hook into the ch made in the last stitch, YO and pull through one loop (1ch made), YO and pull through all three loops on hook; repeat from ★ until you have required number of stitches.

Cable Pattern for Front and Hood

(Worked over ten stitches)
Cable Row 1 (RS): 2RhtrF, 1htr, 4RttrF in the stitches 2 rows below, 1htr, 2RhtrF.
Cable Row 2 (WS): 2RhtrB, 6htr, 2RhtrB.
Cable Row 3: 2RhtrF, 1htr, miss 2, [1RttrF into RttrF 2 rows below] twice,

1RttrF into 1st missed RttrF 2 rows below, 1RttrF into next missed RttrF 2 rows below, 1htr, 1RhtrF.
Cable Row 4: Repeat row 2.
Cable Rows 5–6: Repeat rows 1–2.

PATTERN NOTES:

• The cardigan is mostly seamless, worked from the top of the hood down.
• Instructions are available for boy (buttons on right) and girl (buttons on left) versions.

INSTRUCTIONS:

Hood (All Sizes)

Make 12fhtr.
Set-up Row (WS): 2ch (counts as 1htr), 10htr, make 4htr stitches into the last stitch turning as you go to work into the other side of the fhtr, 11htr, turn. (26) sts.
Row 1(RS): 2ch, work Row 1 of the Cable Pattern (working the RttrF stitches into the fhtr of the foundation) [2htr in htr (worked into the stitch as normal, not the space as in shtr)] four times, work Row 1 of the Cable Pattern (working the RttrF sts into the fhtr of the foundation) 1htr. Turn. (30) sts.
Row 2: 2ch, work Row 2 of the Cable Pattern, [2htr in htr, 1shtr] four times, work Row 2 of the Cable Pattern, 1htr. (34) sts.
Row 3: 2ch, work Row 3 of the Cable Pattern, [2shtr, 2htr in htr] four times, work Row 3 of the Cable Pattern, 1htr. (38) sts.
Row 4: 2ch, work Row 4 of the Cable Pattern, [2htr in htr, 3shtr] four times,

work Row 4 of the Cable Pattern, 1htr. (42) sts.
Row 5: 2ch, work Row 5 of the Cable Pattern, [4shtr, 2htr in htr] four times, work Row 5 of the Cable Pattern, 1htr. (46) sts.
Row 6: 2ch, work Row 6 of the Cable Pattern, [2htr in htr, 5shtr] four times, work Row 6 of the Cable Pattern, 1htr. 50 (50, 50, 50, 50, 50) sts.

For 3 months size, go to row 12.

For sizes 6 months, 1 year, 2 years, 4 years and 6 years ONLY

Row 7: 2ch, work Cable Pattern in established pattern, [6shtr, 2htr in htr] four times, work Cable Pattern in established pattern, 1htr. - (54, 54, 54, 54, 54) sts.

For 6 months size, go to row 12.

For sizes 1 year, 2 years, 4 years and 6 years ONLY

Row 8: 2ch, work Cable Pattern in established pattern, [2htr in htr, 7shtr] four times, work Cable Pattern in established pattern, 1htr. - (-, 58, 58, 58, 58) sts.

For 1 year size, go to row 12.

For sizes 2 years, 4 years and 6 years ONLY

Row 9: 2ch, work Cable Pattern in established pattern, [8shtr, 2htr in htr] four times, work Cable Pattern in established pattern, 1htr. - (-, -, 62, 62, 62) sts.

For 2 years size, go to row 12.

For sizes 4 years and 6 years ONLY
Row 10: 2ch, work Cable Pattern in established pattern, [2htr in htr, 9shtr] four times, work Cable Pattern in established pattern, 1htr. – (-, -, -, 66, 66) sts.

For 4 years size, go to row 12.

For size 6 years ONLY
Row 11: 2ch, work Cable Pattern in established pattern, [10shtr, 2htr in htr] four times, work Cable Pattern in established pattern, 1htr. – (-, -, -, -, 70) sts.

For ALL sizes
Rows 12–18 (23, 24, 26, 27, 29): 2ch, work Cable Pattern in established pattern, 28 (32, 36, 40, 44, 48)shtr, work Cable Pattern in established pattern, 1htr. 50 (54, 58, 62, 66, 70) sts.
Row 19 (24, 25, 27, 28, 30): 2ch, work

Cable Pattern in established pattern, work in shtr making 5shtr2tog evenly spaced across the row, work Cable Pattern in established pattern, 1htr. 45 (49, 53, 57, 61, 65) sts.
Row 20 (25, 26, 28, 29, 31): 2ch, work Cable Pattern in established pattern, 23 (27, 31, 35, 39, 43)shtr, work Cable Pattern in established pattern, 1htr. 45 (49, 53, 57, 61, 65) sts.
Row 21 (26, 27, 29, 30, 32): 2ch, work Cable Pattern in established pattern, work in shtr making 5 (4, 3, 1, 4, 5) shtr2tog evenly spaced across the row, work Cable Pattern in established pattern, 1htr. 40 (45, 50, 56, 57, 60) sts.
Rows 22 (27, 28, 30, 31, 33) – 23 (29, 33, 37, 43, 43): 2ch, work Cable Pattern in established pattern, 18 (23, 28, 34, 35, 38)shtr, work Cable Pattern in established pattern, 1htr. 40 (45, 50, 56, 57, 60) sts.

For size 6 years ONLY
Row 44: 2ch, work Cable Pattern in

established pattern, make 3shtr2tog evenly spaced across the row, work Cable Pattern in established pattern, 1htr. - (-, -, -, -, 57) sts.

Row 45: 2ch, work Cable Pattern in established pattern, 35htr, work Cable Pattern in established pattern, 1htr. - (-, -, -, -, 57) sts.

Neck to Armhole

Row 1 (RS): 2ch, work Cable Pattern for the Front and Hood in established pattern, 0 (0, 2, 3, 3, 3)shtr, (1htr, 1ch, 1htr) in shtr, 2 (4, 3, 4, 4, 4)shtr, (1htr, 1ch, 1htr) in shtr, 9 (10, 13, 15, 16, 16) shtr, (1htr, 1ch, 1htr) in shtr, 2 (4, 3, 4, 4, 4)shtr, (1htr, 1ch, 1htr) in shtr, 1 (1, 3, 4, 4, 4)shtr, work Cable Pattern in established pattern, 1htr. 44 (49, 54, 60, 61, 61) sts.

Rows 2–15 (17, 19, 19, 21, 23): 2ch, work Cable Pattern in established pattern, 1shtr in each shtr, (1htr, ch, 1htr) in each chsp for 16 (18, 20, 20, 22, 24) rows. 108 (121, 134, 140, 149, 157) sts.

Row 16 (18, 20, 20, 22, 24): (this row will separate the sleeves from the body) 2ch, work Cable Pattern in established pattern, 10 (11, 14, 15, 16, 17)shtr, 6 (5, 6, 6, 7, 7)fhtr, miss 19 (23, 24, 25, 27, 29), 28 (31, 36, 38, 41, 43)shtr, 6 (5, 6, 6, 7, 7) fhtr, miss 19 (23, 24, 25, 27, 29), 10 (11, 14, 15, 16, 17) shtr, work Cable Pattern in established pattern, 1htr. 82 (85, 98, 102, 109, 113) sts.

Rows 17 (19, 21, 21, 23, 25) – 44 (48, 50, 53, 57, 61): Work in established pattern.

Break yarn and weave in ends.

Sleeves (Make 2)

Turn your work at the end of each round.

Round 1: Join yarn in the middle of the fhtr on the chain side, 2ch (counts as 1htr), 24 (27, 29, 30, 33, 35) shtr around. Join with a slst into the top of the 2ch. Turn. 25 (28, 30, 31, 34, 36) sts.

Rounds 2–18 (21, 23, 26, 33, 39): continue working in established pattern.

Round 19 (22, 24, 27, 34, 40): 2ch, miss 1 (-, -, 1, -, -), ★1RtrF, 1RtrB; repeat from ★ to end. Join. Do NOT turn. 25 (28, 30, 31, 34, 36) sts.

Round 20 (23, 25, 28, 35, 41): 2ch, ★1RtrF, 1RtrB; repeat from ★ to end. Join. Break yarn and weave in ends.

Ears (Make 4)

Ch10.

Row 1: Starting with the 2nd chain from hook, 9dc. Turn (9)dc.

Row 2: 1dc, 1dc2tog, 6dc. Turn. (8)dc.

Row 3: 1dc, 1dc2tog, 5dc. Turn. (7)dc.

Row 4: 1dc, 1dc2tog, 4dc. Turn. (6)dc.

Row 5: 1dc, 1dc2tog, 3dc. Turn. (5)dc.

Row 6: 1dc, 1dc2tog, 2dc. Turn. (4)dc.

Row 7: 1dc, 1dc2tog, 1dc. Turn. (3)dc.

Row 8: 1dc, 1dc2tog. Turn. (2)dc.

Row 9: 1dc2tog. (1)dc.

Break yarn and weave in ends onto one side of the ears.

Hold two triangles together, with the sides with the ends woven in facing each other and all of the corresponding edges lined up. Starting at the corner where the bottom meets the sides, dc up to the point, making a dc on the edge of each row. When you reach the top point of the triangle (dc, 2ch, dc) in the top stitch, dc back down the other side of the triangle. Break off wool, leaving a 20cm tail for sewing.

Using the photo for placement, sew your wolf ears on to the top of the hood. Weave in ends.

Edging and Buttonholes

Join yarn at bottom right front corner, RS facing to work up the front of the jacket.

[dc into the end of each row for 5cm, 4ch, dc in next row (one buttonhole made)] six (six, seven, seven, eight, eight) times.

Continue working dc around the front of the hood.

On the opposite side to the buttonholes, make one single buttonhole, approx. 7.5cm down from the neck.

Continue working dc down the front of the jacket and around the bottom, back to where the yarn was joined. Break yarn and weave in ends.

Using the photo and buttonholes as a guide for placement, sew on buttons on the far side of opposite cable to buttonholes so that the cable overlaps fully.

THE PLAY ROOM

Star Rug
Sleepy Octopus
Bunting Baby Blanket
Black-eyed Susan Baby Blanket
Hobby Horse

STAR RUG

This fresh twist on a traditional rag rug will add
a touch of fun to any nursery.

skill level:
intermediate

Size	One size
Width	130cm
Yarn amounts	322m

MATERIALS:

- Main Colour (MC): 3 x 500g cones of Hooplayarn (recycled jersey cotton), 100m Grey Marl
- Colour A: 1 x 500g cone of Hooplayarn (recycled jersey cotton), 100m Neon Green
- Colour B: 1 x 500g cone of Hooplayarn (recycled jersey cotton), 100m Aqua Blue
- Colour C: 1 x 500g cone of Hooplayarn (recycled jersey cotton), 100m Darkest Blue
- 9mm/M13 Hook

YARN REVIEW:

Made from waste from the textile industry, this jersey T-shirt yarn makes a hard-wearing (and eco-friendly) rug.

YARN ALTERNATIVES:

Zapetti
Idle Hands T-shirt Yarn

TENSION:

Work 10 sts and 2.5 rows in treble crochet to measure 10cm square with a 9mm hook, or size required to obtain tension.

SPECIAL STITCHES:

Modified Shell (ModShell)
(3tr, 1dtr, 3tr) into the same stitch

Double Crochet Three Together (dc3tog)
[Insert hook into next stitch, YO and pull through stitch] three times (four loops on hook), YO and pull through all four loops.

PATTERN NOTES:

Do not turn your work at the end of each round.

INSTRUCTIONS:

Using MC, 1ch (does not count as a stitch), [1dc, 1ch] five times into a magic loop. Join. (5)dc.

Round 1: 1ch (does not count as a stitch), *2dc into dc, 2dc into chsp; repeat from * to end. Join into 1st dc. (20)dc.

Round 2: 1ch (does not count as a stitch, 1dc, [miss 1, (2tr, dtr, 2tr) in dc, miss one, 1dc] four times, miss 1, (2tr, dtr, 2tr) in dc, miss 1, slst into 1st dc. (30) sts.

Round 3: 3ch (counts as 1tr), 1tr, ModShell into dtr, 2tr, 1dc, * 2tr, ModShell into dtr, 2tr, 1dc; repeat from * to end. Join into top of 3ch. Break yarn. (60) sts.

Round 4: Switch to Colour A, 1slst to 1st tr, 3ch (counts as 1tr), 3tr, ModShell into dtr, 4tr, dc3tog, *4tr, ModShell into dtr, 4tr, dc3tog; repeat from * to end. Join into top of 3ch. Break yarn. (80) sts.

Round 5: Switch to Colour B, 1slst to 1st tr, 3ch (counts as 1tr), 5tr, ModShell into dtr, 6tr, dc3tog, *6tr, ModShell into dtr, 6tr, dc3tog; repeat from * to end. Join into top of 3ch. Break yarn. (100) sts.

Round 6: Switch to Colour C, 1slst to 1st tr, 3ch (counts as 1tr), 7tr, ModShell into dtr, 8tr, dc3tog, *8tr, ModShell into dtr, 8tr, dc3tog; repeat from * to end. Join into top of 3ch. Break yarn. (120) sts.

Round 7: Switch to MC, 1slst to 1st tr, 3ch (counts as 1tr), 9tr, ModShell into dtr, 10tr, dc3tog, *10tr, ModShell into dtr, 10tr, dc3tog; repeat from * to end. Join into top of 3ch. (140) sts.

Round 8: 1slst to 1st tr, 3ch (counts as 1tr), 11tr, ModShell into dtr, 12tr, dc3tog, *12tr, ModShell into dtr, 12tr, dc3tog; repeat from * to end. Join into top of 3ch. (160) sts.

Round 9: 1slst to 1st tr, 3ch (counts as 1tr), 13tr, ModShell into dtr, 13tr, dc3tog, *14tr, ModShell into dtr, 14tr, dc3tog; repeat from * to end. Join into top of 3ch. Break yarn. (180) sts.

Round 10: Switch to Colour A, 1slst to 1st tr, 3ch (counts as 1tr), 15tr, ModShell into dtr, 16tr, dc3tog, *16tr, ModShell into dtr, 16tr, dc3tog; repeat from * to end. Join into top of 3ch. Break yarn. (200) sts.

Round 11: Switch to Colour B, 1slst to 1st tr, 3ch (counts as 1tr), 17tr, ModShell into dtr, 18tr, dc3tog, *18tr, ModShell into dtr, 18tr, dc3tog; repeat from * to end. Join into top of 3ch. Break yarn. (220) sts.

Round 12: Switch to Colour C, 1slst to 1st tr, 3ch (counts as 1tr), 19tr, ModShell into dtr, 20tr, dc3tog, *20tr, ModShell into dtr, 20tr, dc3tog; repeat from * to end. Join into top of 3ch. Break yarn. (240) sts.

Round 13: Switch to MC, 1slst to 1st tr, 3ch (counts as 1tr), 21tr, ModShell into dtr, 22tr, dc3tog, *22tr, ModShell into dtr, 22tr, dc3tog; repeat from * to end. Join into top of 3ch. (260) sts.

Round 14: 1slst to 1st tr, 3ch (counts as 1tr), 23tr, ModShell into dtr, 24tr, dc3tog, *24tr, ModShell into dtr, 24tr, dc3tog; repeat from * to end. Join into top of 3ch. (280) sts.

Break yarn and weave in ends with your crochet hook.

SLEEPY OCTOPUS

This is the perfect companion for all the undersea adventures that may occur in dreamland, though be aware: she snores.

skill level: intermediate

Size	One size
Width	46cm
Yarn amounts	340m

MATERIALS:

◎ Main Colour (MC): 9 x 100g balls of Cygnet Seriously Chunky (100 per cent acrylic), 48m Burnt Orange (4888)

◎ Contrast Colour (CC): 1 x 100g ball of Cygnet Seriously Chunky (100 per cent acrylic), 48m Black (217)

◎ 9mm/M13 hook

◎ Toy stuffing or a pillow measuring approximately 46cm across (square will work if you can't find a round one)

◎ 40cm zipper in a co-ordinating colour

◎ Tapestry needle

◎ Sewing needle

◎ Co-ordinating thread

◎ Stitch marker

YARN REVIEW:

Soft and washable, this affordable yarn is a great option for room decorations.

YARN ALTERNATIVES:

Sirdar Big Softie Super Chunky
Cascade Magnum

TENSION:

Work 9 sts and 8 rounds in double crochet to measure 10cm square using a 9mm hook, or size required to obtain tension.

PATTERN NOTES:

This pattern is worked entirely in the round in the amigurumi style, with no seams or turning chains at the start of the rounds. Mark the beginning of your rounds with a stitch marker.

INSTRUCTIONS:

Legs (Make 8)

Using MC, leave a 15cm tail, make 1ch (does not count as a stitch) and 5dc into a magic loop. (5)dc.

Round 1: 5dc.

Round 2: 2dc in dc, 1dc, dc2tog, 1dc. (5)dc.

Rounds 3–13: (it is easiest to work this section in a spiral, rather than keeping track of stitch counts per round) 1dc, 2dc in the middle of the 'V' where you made 2dc in the previous round, 1dc, dc2tog working on either side of the dc2tog of the previous round, 1dc. (5)dc.

Round 14: [2dc in dc] twice, placing stitch marker in 1st dc, 3dc. (7)dc. Move stitch marker into the first stitch of each round.

Round 15: 2dc, [2dc in dc] twice, 3dc. (9)dc.

Round 16: 3dc, [2dc in dc] twice, 4dc. (11)dc.

Rounds 17–21: 11dc.

Round 22: 1dc, dc2tog, 6dc, dc2tog. (9)dc.

Round 23: dc2tog, 3dc, 2dc in dc, 3dc. (9)dc.

Round 24: dc2tog, 7dc. (8)dc.

Rounds 25–28: 8dc.

Thread the beginning tail onto a tapestry needle. Weave the yarn up through the stitches on the side of the leg that naturally curls in, pulling gently as you go to accentuate the curve of the leg. Once you reach the increase section, bring yarn to inside of the leg and tie off neatly inside the leg.

Cushion (Makes 2)

Using MC, make 1ch (does not count as a stitch), 6dc into a magic loop. (6)dc.

★2dc in dc; repeat from ★ around. (12)dc.

★2dc in dc, 1dc; repeat from ★ around. (18)dc.

★2dc in dc, 2dc; repeat from ★ around. (24)dc.

★2dc in dc, 3dc; repeat from ★ around. (30)dc.

★2dc in dc, 4dc; repeat from ★ around. (36)dc.

★2dc in dc, 5dc; repeat from ★ around. (42)dc.

★2dc in dc, 6dc; repeat from ★ around. (48)dc.

★2dc in dc, 7dc; repeat from ★ around. (54)dc.

★2dc in dc, 8dc; repeat from ★ around. (60)dc.

★2dc in dc, 9dc; repeat from ★ around. (66)dc.

★2dc in dc, 10dc; repeat from ★ around. (72)dc.

★2dc in dc, 11dc; repeat from ★ around. (78)dc.

★2dc in dc, 12dc; repeat from ★ around. (84)dc.

★2dc in dc, 13dc; repeat from ★ around. (90)dc.

★2dc in dc, 14dc; repeat from ★ around. (96)dc.

★2dc in dc, 15dc; repeat from ★ around. (102)dc.

★2dc in dc, 16dc; repeat from ★ around. (108)dc.

Joining

You will slst around the edges. Place the top and bottom pieces, wrong sides together, stitches aligned. Top side facing, make 2slst working through both layers (all four loops) to join the sides together.

Joining with Legs

Fold the open end of tentacle in half, stitches aligned, place it between the two layers of the cushion.

Insert hook through top layer, then insert hook through both layers of the tentacle, then through the bottom side of the cushion.

YO and pull through all layers of stitches until you are at the top and then through the loop on the hook.

Repeat steps 2–3 for the 3 remaining stitches of the leg, then make 3slst, working through both layers of the cushion.

Repeat steps 1–4 for the three remaining legs on that side.

Make 15 slst working through both layers of the cushion.

Repeat steps 1–4 for three legs on the other side of the pillow.

Repeat steps 1-4 for the final leg, but make only 2slst after the final leg. Break yarn and weave in ends.

Insert zipper into opening of the pillow. Using a sewing needle, hand sew one side of the zipper to the upper side of the pillow and one side to the lower side of the pillow, opening the zipper as needed. Stuff cushion with toy stuffing or pillow.

Note: if you don't want to add a zipper, simply slst the pillow closed. (108)slst.

Eyes

Using the photo as a guide, thread a tapestry needle with CC. Embroider the eyes using a back stitch (see Techniques and Basic Stitches on page 15) for the eyelid and then five short stitches for the eyelashes.

BUNTING BABY BLANKET

The bright colours of strung bunting will liven up any nursery.

skill level: intermediate

Size	One size
Finished length	128.5cm
Finished width	88cm
Main colour	1475m
Colour B	185m
Colour C, D, E, F, G	95m

MATERIALS:

- Main Colour (MC): 12 x 50g balls of Milla Mia DK (100 per cent superwash merino wool), 125m Snow (124)
- Colour B: 2 x 50g balls of Milla Mia DK (100 per cent superwash merino wool), 125m Storm (102)
- Colour C: 1 x 50g ball of Milla Mia DK (100 per cent superwash merino wool), 125m Scarlet (140)
- Colour D: 1 x 50g ball of Milla Mia DK (100 per cent superwash merino wool), 125m Daisy (142)
- Colour E: 1 x 50g ball of Milla Mia DK (100 per cent superwash merino wool), 125m Grass (141)
- Colour F: 1 x 50g ball of Milla Mia DK (100 per cent superwash merino wool), 125m Peacock (144)
- Colour G: 1 x 50g ball of Milla Mia DK (100 per cent superwash merino wool), 125m Fuchsia (143)
- 4mm/G6 hook
- Tapestry needle

YARN ALTERNATIVES:
Rowan Pure Wool DK
Patons Fab DK

TENSION:
Work 18sts and 18 rows in dc to measure 10cm square using 4mm hook, or size required to obtain tension.

PATTERN NOTES:

• This pattern is a colourwork/tapestry crochet pattern. To ensure the neatest finish possible, you will carry MC across the coloured bunting triangles by holding it on top of the stitches in the previous row and crocheting around it with your working yarn. This is also a useful method to deal with your wool ends without having to weave them in later.

• You will drop each other colour when you switch to the MC in between each flag. You will leave it hanging and pick it up when you come to it on the next row.

• You will always switch colours when you have two loops from your previous dc on your hook (see Techniques and Basic Stitches on page 14). Do not count the 1ch at the beginning of the row as a stitch.

INSTRUCTIONS:

Using MC, make 157ch.

Row 1: starting with 2nd chain from hook, 156dc. Turn. (156)dc.

Rows 2–4: 1ch. dc across. Turn. (156)dc.

Rows 5–6: switch to Colour B. 1ch. dc across. Turn.

Row 7: (You will need two separate balls of Colour F in this row for two half flags.) Join Colour F. 1ch, 12dc. Switch to MC, 1dc. Switch to Colour E, 25dc. Switch to MC, 1dc. Switch to Colour D, 25dc. Switch to MC, 1dc. Switch to Colour C, 25dc. Switch to MC, 1dc. Switch to Colour B, 25dc. Switch to MC, 1dc. Switch to Colour G, 25dc. Switch to MC, 1dc. Switch to Colour F, 13dc. Turn.

Row 8: In Colour F, 1ch, 12dc. Switch to MC, 3dc. Switch to Colour G, 23dc. Switch to MC, 3dc. Switch to Colour B, 23dc. Switch to MC, 3dc. Switch to Colour C, 23dc. Switch to MC, 3dc. Switch to Colour D, 23dc. Switch to MC, 3dc. Switch to Colour E, 23dc. Switch to MC, 3dc. Switch to Colour F, 11dc. Turn.

Row 9: In Colour F, 1ch, 11dc. Switch to MC, 3dc. Switch to Colour E, 23dc. Switch to MC, 3dc. Switch to Colour D, 23dc. Switch to MC, 3dc. Switch to Colour C, 23dc. Switch to MC, 3dc. Switch to Colour B, 23dc. Switch to MC, 3dc. Switch to Colour G, 23dc. Switch to MC, 3dc. Switch to Colour F, 12dc. Turn.

Row 10: In Colour F, 1ch, 11dc. Switch to MC, 5dc. Switch to Colour G, 21dc. Switch to MC, 5dc. Switch to Colour B, 21dc. Switch to MC, 5dc. Switch to Colour C, 21dc. Switch to MC, 5dc. Switch to Colour D, 21dc. Switch to MC, 5dc. Switch to Colour E, 21dc. Switch to MC, 5dc. Switch to Colour F, 10dc. Turn.

Row 11: In Colour F, 1ch, 10dc. Switch to MC, 5dc. Switch to Colour E, 21dc. Switch to MC, 5dc. Switch to Colour D, 21dc. Switch to MC, 5dc. Switch to Colour C, 21dc. Switch to MC, 5dc. Switch to Colour B, 21dc. Switch to MC, 5dc. Switch to Colour G, 21dc. Switch to MC, 5dc. Switch to Colour F, 11dc. Turn.

Row 12: In Colour F, 1ch, 10dc. Switch to MC, 7dc. Switch to Colour G, 19dc. Switch to MC, 7dc. Switch to Colour B, 19dc. Switch to MC, 7dc. Switch to Colour C, 19dc. Switch to MC, 7dc. Switch to Colour D, 19dc. Switch to MC, 7dc. Switch to Colour E, 19dc. Switch to MC, 7dc. Switch to Colour F, 9dc. Turn.

Row 13: In Colour F, 1ch, 9dc. Switch to MC, 7dc. Switch to Colour E, 19dc. Switch to MC, 7dc. Switch to Colour D, 19dc. Switch to MC, 7dc. Switch to Colour C, 19dc. Switch to MC, 7dc. Switch to Colour B, 19dc. Switch to MC, 7dc. Switch to Colour G, 19dc. Switch to MC, 7dc. Switch to Colour F, 10dc. Turn.

Row 14: In Colour F, 1ch, 9dc. Switch to MC, 9dc. Switch to Colour G, 17dc. Switch to MC, 9dc. Switch to Colour B, 17dc. Switch to MC, 9dc. Switch to Colour C, 17dc. Switch to MC, 9dc. Switch to Colour D, 17dc. Switch to

MC, 9dc. Switch to Colour E, 17dc. Switch to MC, 9dc. Switch to Colour F, 8dc. Turn.

Row 15: In Colour F, 1ch, 8dc. Switch to MC, 9dc. Switch to Colour E, 17dc. Switch to MC, 9dc. Switch to Colour D, 17dc. Switch to MC, 9dc. Switch to Colour C, 17dc. Switch to MC, 9dc. Switch to Colour B, 17dc. Switch to MC, 9dc. Switch to Colour G, 17dc. Switch to MC, 9dc. Switch to Colour F, 9dc. Turn.

Row 16: In Colour F, 1ch, 8dc. Switch to MC, 11dc. Switch to Colour G, 15dc. Switch to MC, 11dc. Switch to Colour B, 15dc. Switch to MC, 11dc. Switch to Colour C, 15dc. Switch to MC, 11dc. Switch to Colour D, 15dc. Switch to MC, 11dc. Switch to Colour E, 15dc. Switch to MC, 11dc. Switch to Colour F, 7dc. Turn.

Row 17: In Colour F, 1ch, 7dc. Switch to MC, 11dc. Switch to Colour E, 15dc. Switch to MC, 11dc. Switch to Colour D, 15dc. Switch to MC, 11dc. Switch to Colour C, 15dc. Switch to MC, 11dc. Switch to Colour B, 15dc. Switch to MC, 11dc. Switch to Colour G, 15dc. Switch to MC, 11dc. Switch to Colour F, 8dc. Turn.

Row 18: In Colour F, 1ch, 8dc. Switch to MC, 11dc. Switch to Colour G, 15dc. Switch to MC, 11dc. Switch to Colour B, 15dc. Switch to MC, 11dc. Switch to Colour C, 15dc. Switch to MC, 11dc. Switch to Colour D, 15dc. Switch to MC, 11dc. Switch to Colour E, 15dc. Switch to MC, 11dc. Switch to Colour F, 7dc. Turn.

Row 19: In Colour F, 1ch, 6dc. Switch to MC, 13dc. Switch to Colour E, 13dc. Switch to MC, 13dc. Switch to Colour D, 13dc. Switch to MC, 13dc. Switch to Colour C, 13dc. Switch to MC, 13dc. Switch to Colour B, 13dc. Switch to MC, 13dc. Switch to Colour G, 13dc. Switch to MC, 13dc. Switch to Colour F, 7dc. Turn.

Row 20: In Colour F, 1ch, 7dc. Switch to MC, 13dc. Switch to Colour G, 13dc. Switch to MC, 13dc. Switch to Colour B, 13dc. Switch to MC, 13dc. Switch to Colour C, 13dc. Switch to MC, 13dc.

Switch to Colour D, 13dc. Switch to MC, 13dc. Switch to Colour E, 13dc. Switch to MC, 13dc. Switch to Colour F, 6dc. Turn.

Row 21: In Colour F, 1ch, 5dc. Switch to MC, 15dc. Switch to Colour E, 11dc. Switch to MC, 15dc. Switch to Colour D, 11dc. Switch to MC, 15dc. Switch to Colour C, 11dc. Switch to MC, 15dc. Switch to Colour B, 11dc. Switch to MC, 15dc. Switch to Colour G, 11dc. Switch to MC, 15dc. Switch to Colour F, 6dc. Turn.

Row 22: In Colour F, 1ch, 6dc. Switch

to MC, 15dc. Switch to Colour G, 11dc. Switch to MC, 15dc. Switch to Colour B, 11dc. Switch to MC, 15dc. Switch to Colour C, 11dc. Switch to MC, 15dc. Switch to Colour D, 11dc. Switch to MC, 15dc. Switch to Colour E, 11dc. Switch to MC, 15dc. Switch to Colour F, 5dc. Turn.

Row 23: In Colour F, 1ch, 4dc. Switch to MC, 17dc. Switch to Colour E, 9dc. Switch to MC, 17dc. Switch to Colour D, 9dc. Switch to MC, 17dc. Switch to Colour C, 9dc. Switch to MC, 17dc. Switch to Colour B, 9dc. Switch to MC, 17dc. Switch to Colour G, 9dc. Switch to MC, 15dc. Switch to Colour F, 5dc. Turn.

Row 24: In Colour F, 1ch, 5dc. Switch to MC, 17dc. Switch to Colour G, 9dc. Switch to MC, 17dc. Switch to Colour B, 9dc. Switch to MC, 17dc. Switch to Colour C, 9dc. Switch to MC, 17dc. Switch to Colour D, 9dc. Switch to MC, 17dc. Switch to Colour E, 9dc. Switch to MC, 17dc. Switch to Colour F, 4dc. Turn.

Row 25: In Colour F, 1ch, 3dc. Switch to MC, 19dc. Switch to Colour E, 7dc. Switch to MC, 19dc. Switch to Colour D, 7dc. Switch to MC, 19dc. Switch to Colour C, 7dc. Switch to MC, 19dc. Switch to Colour B, 7dc. Switch to MC, 19dc. Switch to Colour G, 7dc. Switch to MC, 19dc. Switch to Colour F, 4dc. Turn.

Row 26: In Colour F, 1ch, 4dc. Switch to MC, 19dc. Switch to Colour G, 7dc. Switch to MC, 19dc. Switch to Colour B, 7dc. Switch to MC, 19dc. Switch to Colour C, 7dc. Switch to MC, 19dc.

Switch to Colour D, 7dc. Switch to MC, 19dc. Switch to Colour E, 7dc. Switch to MC, 19dc. Switch to Colour F, 3dc. Turn.

Row 27: In Colour F, 1ch, 2dc. Switch to MC, 21dc. Switch to Colour E, 5dc. Switch to MC, 21dc. Switch to Colour D, 5dc. Switch to MC, 21dc. Switch to Colour C, 5dc. Switch to MC, 21dc. Switch to Colour B, 5dc. Switch to MC, 21dc. Switch to Colour G, 5dc. Switch to MC, 21dc. Switch to Colour F, 3dc. Turn.

Row 28: In Colour F, 1ch, 3dc. Switch to MC, 21dc. Switch to Colour G, 5dc. Switch to MC, 21dc. Switch to Colour B, 5dc. Switch to MC, 21dc. Switch to Colour C, 5dc. Switch to MC, 21dc. Switch to Colour D, 5dc. Switch to MC, 21dc. Switch to Colour E, 5dc. Switch to MC, 21dc. Switch to Colour F, 2dc. Turn.

Row 29: In Colour F, 1ch, 1dc. Switch to MC, 23dc. Switch to Colour E, 3dc. Switch to MC, 23dc. Switch to Colour D, 3dc. Switch to MC, 23dc. Switch to Colour C, 3dc. Switch to MC, 23dc. Switch to Colour B, 3dc. Switch to MC, 23dc. Switch to Colour G, 3dc. Switch to MC, 23dc. Switch to Colour F, 2dc. Turn.

Row 30: In Colour F, 1ch, 2dc. Switch to MC, 23dc. Switch to Colour G, 3dc. Switch to MC, 23dc. Switch to Colour B, 3dc. Switch to MC, 23dc. Switch to Colour C, 3dc. Switch to MC, 23dc. Switch to Colour D, 3dc. Switch to MC, 23dc. Switch to Colour E, 3dc. Switch to MC, 23dc. Switch to Colour F, 1dc. Turn.

Row 31: (On this row, break colours as you go.) Switch to MC, 1ch, 25dc.

Switch to Colour E, 1dc. Switch to MC, 25dc. Switch to Colour D, 1dc. Switch to MC, 25dc. Switch to Colour C, 1dc. Switch to MC, 25dc. Switch to Colour B, 1dc. Switch to MC, 25dc. Switch to Colour G, 1dc. Switch to MC, 25dc. Switch to Colour F, 1dc. Turn.

Rows 32–45: Switch to MC. 1ch. dc across. Turn.

Row 46: In MC, 1ch, 13dc. Switch to Colour C, 1dc. Switch to MC, 25dc. Switch to Colour D, 1dc. Switch to MC, 25dc. Switch to Colour E, 1dc. Switch to MC, 25dc. Switch to Colour F, 1dc. Switch to MC, 25dc. Switch to Colour G, 1dc. Switch to MC, 25dc. Switch to Colour B, 1dc. Switch to MC, 12dc. Turn.

Row 47: In MC, 1ch, 11dc. Switch to Colour B, 3dc. Switch to MC, 23dc. Switch to Colour G, 3dc. Switch to MC, 23dc. Switch to Colour F, 3dc. Switch to MC, 23dc. Switch to Colour E, 3dc. Switch to MC, 23dc. Switch to Colour D, 3dc. Switch to MC, 23dc. Switch to Colour C, 3dc. Switch to MC, 12dc. Turn.

Row 48: In MC, 1ch, 12dc. Switch to Colour C, 3dc. Switch to MC, 23dc. Switch to Colour D, 3dc. Switch to MC, 23dc. Switch to Colour E, 3dc. Switch to MC, 23dc. Switch to Colour F, 3dc. Switch to MC, 23dc. Switch to Colour G, 3dc. Switch to MC, 23dc Switch to Colour B, 3dc. Switch to MC, 11dc. Turn.

Row 49: In MC, 1ch, 10dc. Switch to Colour B, 5dc. Switch to MC, 21dc.

Switch to Colour G, 5dc. Switch to MC, 21dc. Switch to Colour F, 5dc. Switch to MC, 21dc. Switch to Colour E, 5dc. Switch to MC, 21dc. Switch to Colour D, 5dc. Switch to MC, 21dc. Switch to Colour C, 5dc. Switch to MC, 11dc. Turn.

Row 50: In MC, 1ch, 11dc. Switch to Colour C, 5dc. Switch to MC, 21dc. Switch to Colour D, 5dc. Switch to MC, 21dc. Switch to Colour E, 5dc. Switch to MC, 21dc. Switch to Colour F, 5dc. Switch to MC, 21dc. Switch to Colour G, 5dc. Switch to MC, 21dc. Switch to Colour B, 5dc. Switch to MC, 10dc. Turn.

Row 51: In MC, 1ch, 9dc. Switch to Colour B, 7dc. Switch to MC, 19dc. Switch to Colour G, 7dc. Switch to MC, 19dc. Switch to Colour F, 7dc. Switch to MC, 19dc. Switch to Colour E, 7dc. Switch to MC, 19dc. Switch to Colour D, 7dc. Switch to MC, 19dc. Switch to Colour C, 7dc. Switch to MC, 10dc. Turn.

Row 52: In MC, 1ch, 10dc. Switch to Colour C, 7dc. Switch to MC, 19dc. Switch to Colour D, 7dc. Switch to MC, 19dc. Switch to Colour E, 7dc. Switch to MC, 19dc. Switch to Colour F, 7dc. Switch to MC, 19dc. Switch to Colour G, 7dc. Switch to MC, 19dc. Switch to Colour B, 7dc. Switch to MC, 9dc. Turn.

Row 53: In MC, 1ch, 8dc. Switch to Colour B, 9dc. Switch to MC, 17dc. Switch to Colour G, 9dc. Switch to MC, 17dc. Switch to Colour F, 9dc. Switch to MC, 17dc. Switch to Colour E, 9dc. Switch to MC, 17dc. Switch to Colour

D, 9dc. Switch to MC, 17dc. Switch to Colour C, 9dc. Switch to MC, 9dc. Turn.

Row 54: In MC, 1ch, 9dc. Switch to Colour C, 9dc. Switch to MC, 17dc. Switch to Colour D, 9dc. Switch to MC, 17dc. Switch to Colour E, 9dc. Switch to MC, 17dc. Switch to Colour F, 9dc. Switch to MC, 17dc. Switch to Colour G, 9dc. Switch to MC, 17dc. Switch to Colour B. 9dc. Switch to MC, 8dc. Turn.

Row 55: In MC, 1ch, 7dc. Switch to Colour B, 11dc. Switch to MC, 15dc. Switch to Colour G, 11dc. Switch to MC, 15dc. Switch to Colour F, 11dc. Switch to MC, 15dc. Switch to Colour E, 11dc. Switch to MC, 15dc. Switch to Colour D, 11dc. Switch to MC, 15dc. Switch to Colour C, 11dc. Switch to MC, 8dc. Turn.

Row 56: In MC, 1ch, 8dc. Switch to Colour C, 11dc. Switch to MC, 15dc. Switch to Colour D, 11dc. Switch to MC, 15dc. Switch to Colour E, 11dc. Switch to MC, 15dc. Switch to Colour F, 11dc. Switch to MC, 15dc. Switch to Colour G, 11dc. Switch to MC, 15dc Switch to Colour B, 11dc. Switch to MC, 7dc. Turn.

Row 57: In MC, 1ch, 6dc. Switch to Colour B, 13dc. Switch to MC, 13dc. Switch to Colour G, 13dc. Switch to MC, 13dc. Switch to Colour F, 13dc. Switch to MC, 13dc. Switch to Colour E, 13dc. Switch to MC, 13dc. Switch to Colour D, 13dc. Switch to MC, 13dc. Switch to Colour C, 13dc. Switch to MC, 7dc. Turn.

Row 58: In MC, 1ch, 7dc. Switch to Colour C, 13dc. Switch to MC, 13dc.

Switch to Colour D, 13dc. Switch to MC, 13dc. Switch to Colour E, 13dc. Switch to MC, 13dc. Switch to Colour F, 13dc. Switch to MC, 13dc. Switch to Colour G, 13dc. Switch to MC, 13dc. Switch to Colour B, 13dc. Switch to MC, 6dc. Turn.

Row 59: In MC, 1ch, 5dc. Switch to Colour B, 15dc. Switch to MC, 11dc. Switch to Colour G, 15dc. Switch to MC, 11dc. Switch to Colour F, 15dc. Switch to MC, 11dc. Switch to Colour E. 15dc. Switch to MC, 11dc. Switch to Colour D, 15dc. Switch to MC, 11dc. Switch to Colour C, 15dc. Switch to MC, 6dc. Turn.

Row 60: In MC, 1ch, 6dc. Switch to Colour C, 15dc. Switch to MC, 11dc. Switch to Colour D, 15dc. Switch to MC, 11dc. Switch to Colour E, 15dc.

Switch to MC, 11dc. Switch to Colour F, 15dc. Switch to MC, 11dc. Switch to Colour G, 15dc. Switch to MC, 11dc. Switch to Colour B, 15dc. Switch to MC, 5dc. Turn.

Row 61: In MC, 1ch, 5dc. Switch to Colour B, 15dc. Switch to MC, 11dc. Switch to Colour G, 15dc. Switch to MC, 11dc. Switch to Colour F, 15dc. Switch to MC, 11dc. Switch to Colour E, 15dc. Switch to MC, 11dc. Switch to Colour D, 15dc. Switch to MC, 11dc. Switch to Colour C, 15dc. Switch to MC, 6dc. Turn.

Row 62: In MC, 1ch, 5dc. Switch to Colour C, 17dc. Switch to MC, 9dc. Switch to Colour D, 17dc. Switch to MC, 9dc. Switch to Colour E, 17dc. Switch to MC, 9dc. Switch to Colour F, 17dc. Switch to MC, 9dc. Switch to Colour G, 17dc. Switch to MC, 9dc. Switch to Colour B, 17dc. Switch to MC, 4dc. Turn.

Row 63: In MC, 1ch, 4dc. Switch to Colour B, 17dc. Switch to MC, 9dc. Switch to Colour G, 17dc. Switch to MC, 9dc. Switch to Colour F, 17dc. Switch to MC, 9dc. Switch to Colour E, 17dc. Switch to MC, 9dc. Switch to Colour D, 17dc. Switch to MC, 9dc. Switch to Colour C, 17dc. Switch to MC, 5dc. Turn.

Row 64: In MC, 1ch, 4dc. Switch to Colour C, 19dc. Switch to MC, 7dc. Switch to Colour D, 19dc. Switch to MC, 7dc. Switch to Colour E, 19dc. Switch to MC, 7dc. Switch to Colour F, 19dc. Switch to MC, 7dc. Switch to Colour G, 19dc. Switch to MC, 7dc.

Switch to Colour B, 19dc. Switch to MC, 3dc. Turn.

Row 65: In MC, 1ch, 3dc. Switch to Colour B, 19dc. Switch to MC, 7dc. Switch to Colour G, 19dc. Switch to MC, 7dc. Switch to Colour F, 19dc. Switch to MC, 7dc. Switch to Colour E, 19dc. Switch to MC, 7dc. Switch to Colour D, 19dc. Switch to MC, 7dc. Switch to Colour C, 19dc. Switch to MC, 4dc. Turn.

Row 66: In MC, 1ch, 3dc. Switch to Colour C, 21dc. Switch to MC, 5dc. Switch to Colour D, 21dc. Switch to MC, 5dc. Switch to Colour E, 21dc. Switch to MC, 5dc. Switch to Colour F, 21dc. Switch to MC, 5dc. Switch to Colour G, 21dc. Switch to MC, 5dc. Switch to Colour B, 21dc. Switch to MC, 2dc. Turn.

Row 67: In MC, 1ch, 2dc. Switch to Colour B, 21dc. Switch to MC, 5dc. Switch to Colour G, 21dc. Switch to MC, 5dc. Switch to Colour F, 21dc. Switch to MC, 5dc. Switch to Colour E, 21dc. Switch to MC, 5dc. Switch to Colour D, 21dc. Switch to MC, 5dc. Switch to Colour C, 21dc. Switch to MC, 3dc. Turn.

Row 68: In MC, 1ch, 2dc. Switch to Colour C, 23dc. Switch to MC, 3dc. Switch to Colour D, 23dc. Switch to MC, 3dc. Switch to Colour E, 23dc. Switch to MC, 3dc. Switch to Colour F, 23dc. Switch to MC, 3dc. Switch to Colour G, 23dc. Switch to MC, 3dc. Switch to Colour B, 23dc. Switch to MC, dc. Turn.

Row 69: In MC, 1ch, dc. Switch to

Colour B, 23dc. Switch to MC, 3dc. Switch to Colour G, 23dc. Switch to MC, 3dc. Switch to Colour F, 23dc. Switch to MC, 3dc. Switch to Colour E, 23dc. Switch to MC, 3dc. Switch to Colour D, 23dc. Switch to MC, 3dc. Switch to Colour C, 23dc. Switch to MC, 2dc. Turn.

Row 70: (On this row, break colours as you go.) In MC, 1ch, 1dc. Switch to Colour C, 25dc. Switch to MC, 1dc. Switch to Colour D, 25dc. Switch to MC, 1dc. Switch to Colour E, 25dc. Switch to MC, 1dc. Switch to Colour F, 25dc. Switch to MC, 1dc. Switch to Colour G, 25dc. Switch to MC, 1dc. Switch to Colour B, 25dc. Turn.

Rows 71–72: Continuing in Colour B. 1ch, dc across. Break Colour B. Turn.

Rows 73–76: Switch to MC. 1ch, dc across. Turn.

Repeat rows 1–76 twice more.

Bind off and weave in any additional ends.

BLACK-EYED SUSAN BABY BLANKET

The Black-eyed Susan has always been my favourite flower. Bright and sunny, they grow in abundance on the roadsides of my native Iowa. This baby blanket is a very quick and very simple make, easily crocheted in front of a film for a last-minute gift, bringing these happy daisies into any nursery.

skill level: beginner

Size	One size
Finished diameter	84cm
Yarn amounts	243m

MATERIALS:

- Main Colour (MC): 2 x 250g hanks Cascade Yarns Magnum (100 per cent wool), 112m Gold (9463B)
- Contrast Colour (CC): 1 x 250g hank Cascade Yarns Magnum (100 per cent wool), 112m Black (0050)
- 12mm hook
- Tapestry needle

YARN REVIEW:

A lovely single-ply wool in a very thick super-chunky weight means this project flies off the hook.

YARN ALTERNATIVES:

Seriously Chunky by Cygnet

TENSION:

Work 7.25sts and 3.25 rounds in treble crochet to measure 10cm square using a 12mm hook, or size required to obtain tension.

SPECIAL STITCHES:

Treble 3 Together (tr3tog)
YO, insert hook into first stitch to decrease, YO, pull through stitch (three loops on hook). YO, insert hook through the next stitch to decrease, YO and pull through stitch (five loops on hook). YO, insert hook through the 3rd stitch to decrease, YO and pull through stitch (seven loops on hook). YO and pull through six loops. YO, pull through two remaining loops. 2sts decreased.

Pattern notes: Constructed from the centre out
in a circle, the spaces created by the chain stitches
show off the petals of the flower.
Do not turn your work at the end of each round.

INSTRUCTIONS:

Using CC, 1ch (does not count as a stitch), 6dc into a magic loop. Join. (6)dc.

Round 1: 1ch, 2dc into each stitch around. Join. (12)dc.

Round 2: 1ch, ★2dc into the same stitch, 1dc; repeat from ★ to end. Join. (18)dc.

Round 3: 1ch, ★2dc into the same stitch, 2dc; repeat from ★ to end. Join. (24)dc.

Round 4: 4ch (counts as 1dc and 3ch), miss 2, ★1dc, 3ch, miss 2; repeat from ★ to end. Join. Break yarn. (12)dc.

From here forward each 3ch at the beginning of the round counts as a 1tr.

Round 5: (this round is worked into the 3chsp), join MC into the first chsp, 3ch, 3tr, 1ch, ★4tr into the next 3chsp, 1ch; repeat from ★ to end. Join into the top of the 3ch at the beginning of the round. (48)tr.

Round 6: 3ch, [2tr in tr] twice, 1tr, 1ch, miss 1chsp, ★1tr [2tr in tr] twice, 1tr, 1ch, miss ch; repeat from ★ to end. Join. (72)tr.

Round 7: 3ch, 1tr, 2tr in tr, 3tr, 1ch, miss 1chsp, ★2tr, 2tr in tr, 3tr, 1ch, miss 1chsp; repeat from ★ to end. Join. (84)tr.

Round 8: 3ch, 2tr, 2tr in tr, 3tr, 1ch, miss 1chsp, ★3tr, 2tr in tr, 3tr, 1ch, miss 1chsp; repeat from ★ to end. Join. (96)tr.

Round 9: 3ch, 3tr, 2tr in tr, 3tr, 1ch, miss 1chsp, ★4tr, 2tr in tr, 3tr, 1ch, miss 1chsp; repeat from ★ to end. Join. (108)tr.

Round 10: 3ch, miss 1tr, 5tr, tr2tog, 3ch, miss 1chsp, ★tr2tog, 5tr, tr2tog, 3ch, miss 1chsp; repeat from ★ to end. Join. (84)tr.

Round 11: 3ch, miss 1tr, 3tr, tr2tog, 1ch, 3tr into 3chsp, 1ch, ★tr2tog, 3tr, tr2tog, 1ch, 3tr into 3chsp, ch; repeat from ★ to end. Join. (96)tr.

Round 12: 3ch, miss 1tr, 1tr, tr2tog, 1ch, miss 1chsp, 2tr in tr, 1tr, 2tr in tr, 1ch, miss 1chsp, ★tr2tog, 1tr, tr2tog, 1ch, miss 1chsp, 2tr in tr, 1tr, 2tr in tr, 1ch, miss 1chsp; repeat from ★ to end. Join. (96)tr.

Round 13: 3ch, tr2tog, 1ch, miss 1chsp, 2tr in tr, 2ch, miss 1tr, 2tr in tr, 2ch, miss 1tr, 2tr in tr, 1ch, miss 1tr, ★tr3tog, 1ch, miss 1chsp, 2tr in tr, 2ch, miss 1tr, 2tr in tr, 2ch, miss 1tr, 2tr in tr, 1ch, miss 1chsp; repeat from ★ to end. Join. (84)tr.

Break yarn and weave in ends. The pattern made by the chain spaces will be most visible if the piece is lightly blocked.

HOBBY HORSE

Who doesn't love whizzing around the house on a pretend horse?
Hours of fun will be had on this lovely heirloom toy.

skill level: intermediate

Size	One size
Finished measurements (stuffed)	20cm x 25cm
Yarn amounts: Grey Mare	197m
Yarn amounts: Mane	71m
Yarn amounts: Unicorn	213m

MATERIALS:

For Grey Mare
- Main Colour (MC): 2 x 50g balls of Wendy Mode DK (50 per cent wool, 50 per cent acrylic), 142m Fog (232)
- Colour A: 1 x 50g ball of Wendy Mode DK (50 per cent wool, 50 per cent acrylic), 142m Shale (219)
- Colour B: 1 x 50g ball of Wendy Mode DK (50 per cent wool, 50 per cent acrylic), 142m Coffee Bean (218)

For Unicorn
- Main Colour (MC): 3 x 50g balls of Wendy Mode DK (50 per cent wool, 50 per cent acrylic), 142m Whisper White (232)

- 4mm/G6 hook
- 3.75mm/F5 hook
- Tapestry needle
- Toy stuffing
- 2 x buttons (2.5cm in diameter) for eyes
- Wooden dowel (1.5cm diameter x 90cm long)
- Linseed or other wood finishing oil
- Small handsaw
- Hot glue (optional)

YARN REVIEW:
Highly durable, but still lovely to work with, this DK-weight 50 per cent wool-acrylic mix is perfect for a well-loved toy that is going to be played with day in day out.

YARN ALTERNATIVES:
Patons Fab DK

TENSION:
Work 16 sts and 13.5 rows in htc to measure 10cm square using a 4mm hook, or size required to obtain tension.

INSTRUCTIONS:

Muzzle

Do not turn your work at the end of each round.

Using the larger hook and the yarn for the nose (Main Colour for Unicorn, Colour A for Grey Mare), 1ch, 8dc into a magic loop. Join. (8)dc.

Round 1: 1ch, ★2dc into dc; repeat from ★ around. Join. (16)dc.

Round 2: 1ch, ★2dc into dc, 1dc; repeat from ★ around. Join. (24)dc.

Round 3: 1ch, ★2dc into dc, 2dc; repeat from ★ around. Join. (32)dc.

Round 4: 1ch, ★2dc into dc, 3dc; repeat from ★ around. Join. (40)dc.

Round 5: 1ch, ★2dc into dc, 4dc; repeat from ★ around. Join. (48)dc.

Round 6: 1ch, ★2dc into dc, 5dc; repeat from ★ around. Join. (56)dc.

For the Grey Mare, if you are alternating colours between the nose and the main horse, switch to MC.

This section is worked entirely in the round in the amigurumi style, with no seams or turning chains at the start of the rounds.

Rounds 7–33: 56dc. Join. Do not turn. (56)dc.

Top of Head

This section is worked in rows. Turn your work at the end of each row.

Rows 1–14: 1ch, 28dc. Turn. (28)dc.

Fold the last row in half, right sides together lining up the stitches, working through all four loops, 14slst to close the seam. Break yarn.

Pattern notes: For the unicorn, there are no colour changes. The 1ch beginning the rounds and rows in this pattern does not count as a stitch.

Neck

This section is worked entirely in the round in the amigurumi style, with no seams or turning chains at the start of the rounds. Do not turn your work at the end of the round.

Set-up

Rejoin yarn next to where you started working in rows. Work 1dc into the end of each row around the unworked stitches from the muzzle. (56)dc.

Round 1: *dc2tog, 5dc; repeat from * around. (48)dc.

Rounds 2–25: 48dc. (48)dc.

Rounds 26–33: Switch to smaller hook. 2ch (does not count as a stitch) *RtrF, RtrB; repeat from * around. (48) sts.

Ears (Make 4)

With larger hook and MC for Unicorn/ Grey Mare, make 9ch.

Row 1: Starting with the second chain from hook, 8dc. Turn. (8)dc.

Row 2: 1ch, 3dc, dc2tog, 4dc. Turn. (7)dc.

Row 3: 1ch, 2dc, dc2tog, 3dc. Turn. (6)dc.

Row 4: 1ch, 2dc, dc2tog, 2dc. Turn. (5)dc.

Row 5: 1ch, 2dc, dc2tog, 1dc. Turn. (4)dc.

Row 6: 1ch, 2dc, dc2tog. Turn. (3)dc.

Row 7: 1ch, 1dc, dc2tog. Turn. (2)dc.

Row 8: dc2tog. Break yarn. (1)dc.

Hold two ears together, wrong sides facing. Rejoin yarn at the edge of the beginning ch. Working into the ends of the rows, 7dc, [1dc, 2ch, 1dc] into dc2tog from Row 8, 7dc down the other end of the rows. Break yarn, leaving a 20cm tail for sewing on.

Unicorn Horn

This section is worked entirely in the round in the amigurumi style, with no seams or turning chains at the start of the rounds. Do not turn your work at the end of the round.

With the larger hook and the yarn for the horn, 1ch (does not count as a stitch), 4dc into a magic loop. (4)dc.

Round 1: 4dc.

Round 2: *1dc, 2dc into next; repeat from * around. (6)dc.

Round 3: 6dc.

Round 4: *1dc, 2dc into next; repeat from * around. (9)dc.

Round 5: 9dc.

Round 6: *2dc, 2dc into next; repeat from * around. (12)dc.

Rounds 7–11: 12dc.

Break yarn, leaving a 30cm tail for sewing on. Lightly stuff.

Stuffing

Stuff the full length of the head part of your horse with toy stuffing. To help minimise lumps in the horse, try and fill the head with a single piece of stuffing, rather than filling it with small pieces at a time.

Tying Mane

Using Colour A for Grey Mare and MC for Unicorn, cut strips of yarn, roughly 17.5cm in length. Fold the strips in half and, using your crochet hook, pull the loops through the space between the stitches where you want the mane. Thread the ends of the mane strips through the loop and pull tight. Repeat until the mane is as full as you want it to be.

Bridle

Using the larger crochet hook and Colour B for Grey Mare and MC for Unicorn, join yarn at the underside of the muzzle of the horse on the outside of row 17 of the muzzle. Using the space between the stitches as a guide, slst on the outside of the nose around in a full circle.

Using a second length of the same yarn (either a separate length cut from the ball or pulled from the centre of the skein), hold the wool double and make a chain 50cm.

Bring the long end of the reins around

the back and slst to join the reins to the bridle. Weave in ends.

Sewing Up

Using the photo for placement, sew on ears and buttons for eyes. For eyelashes, cut a number of strands of wool and tie around the button. Trim to desired length.

Stick

Follow the instructions on the wood treatment oil to treat your dowel.

Using your handsaw, mark three lines 19cm/20cm/21cm down from the top of the dowel. Saw three notches into the wood, approximately 5mm wide and deep all the way around the dowel at these marks.

Wrap dowel with stuffing to the point of the first notch, and add extra stuffing at the top of the horse's head. Insert dowel into neck of horse. Wrap extra yarn tightly and securely around the outside of the horse's neck repeatedly at the point of the notches to secure it to the horse. (For extra security, you can add a bit of hot glue to the dowel notches before wrapping.)

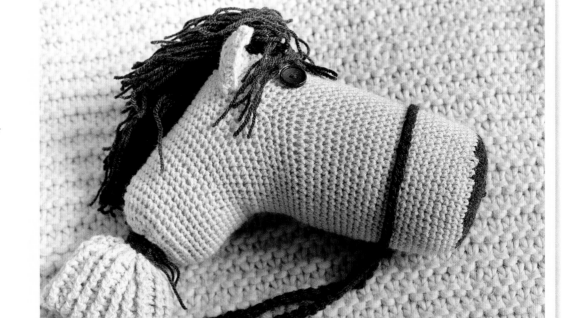

SOURCES FOR SUPPLIES

To find a local source for the yarns used in this book, contact the manufacturers below.

Adriafil Srl
Italian yarn company, offering yarns in a huge range of weights, colours and fibres.
www.adriafil.com/uk

Artesano Ltd.
Makers of Alpaca and merino wools.
www.artesanoyarns.co.uk

Cascade Yarns
Manufacturers of a wide range of wools.
www.cascadeyarns.com

Coats and Crafts
Suppliers of Patons yarns.
www.coatscrafts.co.uk/Products/Knitting

Cygnet Yarns Ltd
UK-based manufacturer of yarn.
www.cygnetyarns.com

Designer Yarns
Providers of Debbie Bliss wools.
www.designeryarns.uk.com

Hooplayarn
Supplier of recycled cotton jersey yarn.
www.hooplayarn.co.uk

Jamieson's
Suppliers of Shetland wool.
www.jamiesonsofshetland.co.uk

Malabrigo Yarn
Providers of a range of wool in beautiful hand-dyed colours.
www.malabrigoyarn.com

Milla Mia
Manufacturers of DK-weight superwash merino wool.
www.millamia.com

Quince and Co.
Gorgeous yarns in a range of subtle colours and variety of weights.
quinceandco.com

Rico Design
A range of beautiful and affordable cotton and wool yarns.
www.rico-design.de

Rowan Yarns
Providers of a huge range of yarns in most weights and fibres.
www.knitrowan.com

Sublime Yarns/Sirdar Spinning Ltd
Manufacturers of both Sublime and Sirdar yarns.
www.sirdar.co.uk

Thomas B. Ramsden (Bradford) Limited
Suppliers of Wendy yarns.
www.tbramsden.co.uk

Yarn Love
Hand-dyed yarns in a huge array of colours and bases.
www.shopyarnlove.com

Zitron
Manufacturers of Trekking Tweed.
www.atelierzitron.de

OTHER CRAFT SUPPLIES

Yarns, Hooks and Other Notions

UK
Loop Knitting
www.loopknittingshop.com

McA Direct
www.mcadirect.com

Australia
Morris and Sons
http://morrisandsons.com.au

The Wool Shack
www.thewoolshack.com

New Zealand
Knit World
www.knitting.co.nz

The Yarn Studio
www.theyarnstudio.co.nz

Wooden and Branch Buttons
Little Woodlanders
http://www.etsy.com/shop/
LittleWoodlanders

Children's clothing for photoshoots

Juicy Tots
www.juicytots.co.uk

Livie & Luca
www.livieandluca.co.uk

Love It Love It Love It
www.loveitloveitloveit.co.uk

Sisters Guild
www.sistersguild.co.uk

Tootsa MacGinty
www.tootsamacginty.com

Wild Things Funky Little Dresses
www.etsy.com/shop/wildthingsdresses

ACKNOWLEDGEMENTS

Every time I pick up a book, the first thing I do is read the acknowledgements. The list of people says so much about the author and the process of bringing a book to life. My list of people is long, with so many people having left their mark on these pages.

Thank you first to my agent, Clare Hulton, whose belief in my work and desire to help left me over the moon at actually landing a deal. In fact, I still can't believe it.

To the wonderful staff at Kyle Books. Having long been a fan of their beautiful books, I am thrilled a work of mine is in the catalogue. Thank you Vicky, Nadine, Louise and all the others who made my book so beautiful.

Thank you to the models and their parents for allowing us to photograph their adorable children in my designs and to the yarn companies who generously gave yarn for use in the book: Artesano, Cascade Yarns, Cygnet, Designer Yarns, Malabrigo Yarns, Milla Mia, and Sublime/Sirdar.

My business partner, Kat Molesworth, for her unending wit and encouragement and for taking over much of the burden of the business while I wrote. She gave me the idea for the book in the first place: thank you!!

My technical editor, Joanne Scrace, deserves the highest praise for taking my patterns and turning them into something that makes sense. Many email and text messages, hundreds of tweets, a lot of brainstorming (the Sleepy Octopus and the Star Rug were her ideas), Joanne's patience and knowledge was a rock that gave me the confidence to design, knowing that she would be there to fix my mistakes.

To my friends, real and 'imaginary', who generously gave ideas, cake and unending support and patience as I dove head first into this huge task. So many people in real life and online pushed me not only to write the best book possible, but to believe that what I have to offer is worth reading, and I can never thank them enough.

My sister-in-law, Jessica Harrison, deserves a huge thank you for her help with sample making, as I would never have finished things in time! The brown Silver Birch Tunic and the Bunting Baby Blanket are her hard work.

To our parents, whose help and guidance supported us through a hectic summer of writing.

My three children, Ellis, Georgia and Theo, who were (mostly) patient while Momma worked. Thank you, Ellis, for your tolerance as I promised yet again that I would play with you in five minutes/after this row/once the book is done. Georgia, thank you for staying relatively still as I measured and fitted and refitted so many different items. And Theo, thank you for only pouring coffee over my computer twice.

Last, and certainly most, Kevin. It is a gift to be with someone who believes in your work so thoroughly that they will make huge sacrifices to make it happen. Thank you doesn't even cover it. I love you, always.